PerpeTraitors

Brian Huff

Chapter I

Forthwith, there are those who disdain the recognized and identifiable illusion: a gross delusion is upon us which is strong from the Lord of hosts. There are many here among us who will wax richer, both good and evil, as the strokes of swords and mightier pens thrust upon the beleaguered minds of the masses with a force of iron-clad will demonstrable to all who would fancy to deem upon the contemporaneous occasions throughout the globe. Aye, the archaic faults have been remonstrated that the establishment was so fond of. Maybe, the path that has been taken few would have chosen with an ultimate hindsight once our history has been cogitated.

Behold, a parsimonious plethora of patients, whom having contracted disease, form "snow-angels" in the dust and ashes of a billowing volcanic hell of misfortune, refusing to pay the exorbitant fees of the medical racket clamoring for your illegal dependence on the government. Enter into the halls of sterilized refinement where once again thou art served with chemicals. Some are condemned by their habitual actions by

physicians whom we are to honor only
requesting the remainder of their dear
fortunes, never to be wisely bestowed upon
grandchildren. Then they are temporarily
spared by pseudo-miraculous medications or
shall we say pharmaceutical sorceries. Then,
farewell, let death overtake the diagnosed
whom rightly possess qualms with sparing
the proportionally minutest expenditure. The
hospital-omniscience after one's blood
sample is forfeited suggests that ye squander
your wealth upon one's very existence like
an extremely expensive telephone call for an
UBER on the river Styx. Whatever prolongs
one's rationale for breathing another day for
a year's salary is logical to the medical
association that sanctions abortion and the
creation of a new gender for emotional
reasons concocted by a client. This railing
will, indubitably, attract negativity as being
disgraceful and a shame. Therefore, edify
yourselves with this beloved text and drink
from the precious fountains created by God,
not the fluoridated water shared with
strangers, to avoid being lulled into the
aforementioned schemes. Care not for what
you drink and find the spring of everlasting
life, the healing Savior, to avoid this
ignorance. Forget the misdoing of your

distant past which will only foster disappointment. Let your life be governed by love, truth, and honor. Take no care for what you eat and fast; responsibility accompanies the consumption of what God has made for mankind: fresh produce. The politest youth will speak before the elderly with few words, will never seek to correct them, and the wisest elders will share their thoughts aloud as the fop who holds his tongue will appear wise.

Always show hospitality to a visitor, but never let a stranger enter one's house lest he venture into something unexpected. There was once a typical man who entered upon a dwelling and when spoken to, revealed he was no angel in disguise, but commenced to hop wildly to and fro, knocked down furniture and escaped out the door in haste, senselessly. These recollections may garner some interest because of their truthfulness. A fiction should have a happy ending, but a work like this may be of a different sort. In order to avoid being a published disturbance, the author shall heretofore observe the established protocols of Western culture. Enjoy the secret inspiration behind this prose of a common magnitude. Picture the Capitol's rotunda as a giant cylinder of a revolver pointing a coup de' tat, rat tat tat, of impeachment bullets at the leader of our people. There are already credentialed specialists who have conducted studies on the President confirming that he is mentally ill with the political motive of his removal from office. A diagnosis by a professional trump's the people's will and the patients, I daresay, despite all obstinacy on the part of the accused. Insignificant is the individual's opinion of the matter when those who are against him point the finger at him, towards his temporal lobe. Forthcoming is the ex nihilo impeachment of the perpetrator of nothing amidst a scandalous renaissance from the depths of demagoguery. The accusations fell when faced with the fortitude of those who resist the Deep State. Contrary to the Communist propaganda of the sensationalized enemy of the people, this prose has been initiated. The Incense and Insensibility of the Communist-hippie movement has burgeoned into an elderly generation expressing Pride in not being Prejudiced. No longer will Mary Jane be illegal in Austin, Texas, but will actually be prescribed to patients under the duress of the professional hierarchy. Being bigoted is not a fine attribute, but the political correctness is boiling over the witch's cauldron and our first born sons need that kind of freeness, that genderless enchantment, man. Then they can be puppets, incapable of being confused, but of course upwardly immobile with strings of debt attached. Innumerable as the stars of heaven and the grains of sand on the sea shore are we now as promised by God. Yet, the master of evil seeks to depopulate the earth in the name of faux-environmentalism like a neo-Stalin. The statesmanship of this progressive leader offered the massacre of millions of Russians for the sake of politics knowing full well that history would repeat itself. The consciousness of all Communist dictators are seething in their victims' blood and roasting in hell. The Leftist is the greatest hypocrite, enjoying the appearance of benevolence while denying omnipotence. First, Satan's strawman was the ruler, then the noblemen, and then the millionaires, all playing upon the jealousy of mankind just as Lucifer was envious of God. Now "the Accuser" or "Adversary" is all but imperceptible, once the Lord asked him what he was doing in the days of Job and the Devil answered that he was roaming the earth, per se. Needless to say, the Bible commands us not to wander through the streets at night, aimlessly; if one is able to draw some sort of connection between the last two notions that would be swell. Perhaps, one may draw a contrast between Stalin and Trump if one would prefer to read left to right or even free oneself from the Leftist guilt of feeling selfish for not desiring higher taxes. There seems to be a prevalence of civil unrest, all coaxed by Leftist agitators who would rob our people of their tranquility and property due to Karl Marx and the guillotine mind-set of the Enlightenment. A knight's armor might seem outdated until one becomes the target of a mob without the right to bear firearms, then a medieval sort of lifestyle could become feasible again without the pollution even, just as long as everything makes perfect sense.

This seems to be the opposition's strategy, to pervert the truth, for the Devil was the father of lies and the First Perpetrator. Tis true that sorrow accompanies much knowledge, but the Bible commands us to actually buy knowledge, so no wonder we spend money on a higher education in Christianized countries. Yet, students are early on ruined by the usury demanded of them through loans. The shrine of secularism bids them to protest all the ideas of our ancestors and to embrace the atheistic curriculum orbiting around the "Manifesto". We are taught nothing scriptural that is not able to be adapted to the "Manifesto", but are entreated by man's wisdom and science, falsely so-called, as the Bible puts it. In the most Christian nation, its adherents are forced to undergo humiliation for their beliefs and adopt quasi-religious views in an attempt to form a consensus, yoked with unbelieving peers. Our society would attempt to forcibly tranquilize Christ Jesus if He attempted to rout anyone like he did the money-changers at the Temple. There are numberless objections that might be made to our system of civilization which are usually forwarded by the extreme wings of both parties. At least, Trump does not wear a mask like others who are politicians, that is what the Antifa terrorists are literally good at while they draw parallels between Nazis and patriotic Americans because, after all, both would fight for their country, so obviously any type of nationalist sentiment should logically be equated, not. Antifa activist, may you be rebuked perpetually for acts unbecoming of a gentleman such as throwing urine and chanting obscenities at normal people with alternate opinions. The President should anticipate another appropriations bill from Congress that leads to an unbalanced budget and should, despite being accused of illegalities, refuse to sign it even if it leads to another government shut-down. That is what the author of "PerpeTraitors" recommended to him in a comments section of a survey taken as a member of the Presidential Advisory Board, sometimes a good storm is needed to wash away all the filth that naturally accumulates in Washington. The author campaigned for him locally and was much surprised by Trump's loyalty to our country after his victory. The election was a cause for much joy and it is the author's opinion that Mr. Trump is the best President since Calvin Coolidge. Our country has been in a down-ward spiral of debt for decades and this tribulation was about to become a catastrophe with no manufacturing jobs and other countries taking an unfair advantage over us. He is being accused of incompetence by the very people who are willing to betray their oath to the

Constitution of the United States. The
President does not mind if business and our
people profit from productivity because he is
a Capitalist who knows that an overbearing
government hampers economic growth and
lowering taxes stimulates the economy. He
is a dauntless leader who went to the United
Nations, the epicenter of globalism and mass
migration policies, and told them each
government should put their own country's
interest first and that if illegal aliens come
over the Southern border, we will send them
back, despite his predecessors who granted
amnesty to millions contrary to our
immigration laws. Our country's inhabitants
now see hope for the war against the drug
cartels and gangs. Trump knows we do not
have to submit to losing our country to
international trade policies that eat away our
very substance. Donald Trump was destined
to lead our people despite these witch-hunts,
those nations who will not follow our lead
shall perish and this is precisely why the
Soviet Union collapsed and became a
democracy espousing Capitalism. The
President already exuded with achievement
before holding the most honorable position
in the land. If it were not for the prohibition
of cruel and unusual punishment, the

radicalized Leftists would literally draw and quarter him, tar and feathering his supporters after a foreseen revolt.

The police are our defense against these anarchists who could foreseeably resort to arson, theft, destruction of property, and even murder. The police force limits their ability to act as "perpetraitors", especially now that they are categorized as a terrorist organization. It is remarkable that the movement has not been laid to rest in its coffin, but it has its enablers in the media and the city governments. Antifa has formed a resistance that engenders strife, disorder, and even chaos against those whom they falsely accuse of Fascism. They believe they can veil their intentions by touting anti-racist rhetoric, but they are for a treasonous overthrow of our government. They have schemed for longer than their public infamy has been displayed and their seeds of corruption were planted by liberal professors in the various departments of the universities who purposefully commit to rejecting Conservatives seeking positions. This was recognized vocally by a Conservative geography professor who warned his students that his kind were being almost persecuted, but luckily he changed this author's life around dramatically for good. Antifa is responsible for inciting violence whenever Conservatives are exercising their freedom of speech, (like the Patriot Prayer group who was designated as racist by Diane Feinstein even though their leader is a minority) and has perpetrated various crimes. Their deliberate means of causing civil unrest are still being protected currently by the same people who are creating sanctuary cities for illegal aliens. Antifa's licentious behavior is not for the good of the community. Cities used to order bans on Elvis Presley records in juke-boxes and now the state of affairs is that we must tolerate masked hooligans armed with rioting gear that force those regular people practicing the right to freedom of assembly to wear helmets and carry shields. They glory in viciously attacking people that are waving the American flag and even journalists. They overwhelmingly are in favor of seeking to depose the President of the United States. This would be a great tragedy for our country, but luckily the Senate will not vote to convict the President of any unwarranted accusations after his impeachment.

The President is in favor of law and order and will not surrender willingly to mob rule. Neither will his compatriots who hold similar beliefs relinquish their rights of freedom of speech and to bear arms even if that means there will be shedding of blood. We have the Constitution on our side, whereas their angst shall be transitory against one man, but unable to withstand a like successor. However destructive the ends will be for their goal to rend the moral fabric of our society, there are just as many guns as there are people in this nation and the military will defect if asked to attack the defenders of traditional values. The election has demonstrated the inadequacy of confining one's political support within the limits of major cities. Any armed conflict between the people of America will re-inforce the vulnerability of these cities who have also ironically outlawed firearms rendering them defenseless; the Left does not even possess the courage to engage! It would be difficult to constrain them from rioting and imagine the population centers without electricity after guerillas attack the power grid. This topic is addressed in all perspicuity about these perpetraitors who shall be hung if they attempt to execute a coup; rebellion is as the sin of witchcraft. They readily insult this country and the pursuit of property claiming inequality and disadvantage as the injustice of modern day society just as Karl Marx. They perceive that they are getting stronger by indoctrinating children with programs such as "Drag Queen Story Hour". Why are not these drag queens smoking while they read books to potential comrades, aka., preschoolers? People would object to that, but not for cross-dressing, even though the Bible is explicit about the latter, but not the former. They would tolerate Satan incarnate, now! Predictably, the Democrats shall suffer a crushing defeat in the polls, yet again. Once the Republicans manage to dominate for any extended period of time, the Democrats will fail as the Federalist's Party did under the power of entrenched incumbency, for their only chance is if the country remains divided due to media propaganda scrutinizing the Right. Either of these two options are inevitable and the Democrats will not be able to raise a mandate from the people without replacing the current population with immigrants over the long term. Foreigners are naturally less loyal to our country and that is why the Constitution does not allow one to become President and elected officials must be residents for a specific duration before holding office. This vision of our future is not as bleak as one might imagine unless one is a Leftist.

The Leftists have never managed to overthrow Capitalism and their only successful approach has been gradualism, certainly. Also, our debt is at an excess and taxes will be unpopular, so the future is now with the Conservatives to take back their losses in history. Trump's victory now overshadows the Deep State and globalism. We should forward our Declaration of Independence to the United Nations, immediately, which has sanctioned Communism and the overthrowing of governments internationally. Zeal for our own people will be aroused once the truth universally comes to light about how much we are being used by other states throughout the world and we shall righteously reject those types of treaties which have previously committed us to ongoing armed conflict, to our own detriment. Merry Christmas America: Donald Trump is fighting the "Perpetraitors", finally. He is not falling for a Doomsday scenario about the environment that is designed to force a prohibition of industry in this country as the Communist judges necessary. Our President has designed a rapprochement with Russia now that it disavows Communism. This provides us with a future protection from a nuclear war instead of just having faith in avoiding mutual annihilation. That is a worthwhile investment: peace because wars are most costly. The Liberal doctrine is now described as "progressive" because the "Perpetraitors" saw that their political philosophy was beginning to be connotatively viewed as negative by the voters. Only, the word progressive is nothing new like its adherents might believe, but is a term that was used over a century ago by politicians who were actually socially Conservative or traditional. Today, Conservatism is really a reflection of being practical when it comes to government expenditures, opposing new methods of exaction from the American people to pay bureaucrats that end up costing trillions of dollars that do not even currently exist to be taxed! We are no longer peasants, the lower class enjoys things that should not be taken for granted here including running water, electricity, automobiles, cell phones, restaurants, etc. Yet, they are being persuaded to hold some sort of conviction against modern civilization itself, however repugnant. Liberty is still not commonplace, so the Left should be more appreciative of what God has provided. Incidentally, a large portion of them wholly reject God's very existence and are pessimistic against our country which incites misanthropy. They will eventually begin to characterize extremely Conservative folks as being akin to lunatics, as they have our Commander-in-Chief.

Chapter II

These "Perpetraitors" against our Republic are a baneful segment of the populace that possess extreme Left-wing views, re-shaping the Democratic Party. Everyone should say a prayer for our leaders, but instead there are literally people practicing witchcraft with voodoo dolls against our President attempting to bind him with spells in occult rituals. Their latest claim for impeachment is that the President abused his power when having a conversation with the Ukranian President, but because of the media bias most do not know that it was in order to investigate a corrupt deal worth millions by the ex-Vice President's son, which Joe Biden bragged about on air. It seems as though there are voluminous scandals perpetrated by Democrats that the propaganda in our country does not even address on television. Propaganda is so powerful in America because the people govern by ballot and now their decisions are based on lies. The next Democrat running for President will not even have to raise half the campaign funds because the news media will already air stories constantly in favor of him. The Conservative movement has suffered from slanted news coverage for decades. This will only get worse now that the President has called them out for it and this propaganda must be eliminated if people are to make fair decisions about politics. Not to mention, these are the same companies that broadcast pornographic and excessively violent evil on television. Still, many viewers remain unconcerned with the amount of de-sensitization they are exposed to through these media outlets. Now the populace is seriously considering legalizing prostitution even and as long as both parties are consenting, all types of sexual immorality are tolerated. One thing that has given a surge to the Conservative movement are the independent or alternative media sites on the internet. These and other organizations do not dilute the facts to conform to a Liberal agenda.

The "Perpetraitors" of the Deep State desire a totally subordinate population that is no longer willing to support liberty, steadfastly. The general government has become a leviathan contrary to the Constitution. Make no mistake, Communists are militant detractors to our Constitutional Republic. This world-view is contagious and has dire consequences. We have heretofore witnessed an ideological invasion from within that has permeated American institutions. The names the "Red Scare" and "McCarthyism" are just cover-ups of what has actually taken place or else why would one third of the youngest generation now view Communism favorably despite it being notorious. There has been an overall increase in state-subsidized activities ever since the Soviets infiltrated our government in the early twentieth-century, as well. People are no longer willing to stand up to adversity because they are aware of the ever increasing negative repercussions. There is all of this misinformation out now about the world's overpopulation, though everyone would fit in the state of New Jersey, and the United Nations has an agenda to decrease the population by sterilization and by exterminating fetuses. Euthanasia schemes and mass migrations into countries of European descent are also part of the diabolical plot of these un-elected, sinister globalists. Some of the "Perpetraitors" represent dictators. Historically, cultural diversity does not bring citizens together and the people of Africa, the Middle East, and Asia want to take advantage of the failing Socialist programs of Western culture. A nation's wealth is based upon its production and yet statistically these immigrants are more dependent on the tax-payers of these countries (including ours) than ever before. Conservatives are not against charity, they just believe the government should not be involved in this line of work due to its inefficiency, corruption, and possible abuse of power.

One reason we need the Southern Border Wall is because of the millions of desperate

South Americans who could flee en masse to our country if something catastrophic happens. Then there might be rebellion. With numerous caravans of thousands at once, who could stop our country from being flooded by immigrants? We have enjoyed political stability since the Civil War, we do not need South American and Central American paupers to over-run our towns who would be susceptible to Communist beliefs. It takes a long time for members of a new demographic to become assimilated to ideas that are foreign to them. We do not want Washington, D.C. to be run Moscow-style. Any argument that overbearing massive amounts of migration would be beneficial would be fallacious. It would result in a negative, permanent, and complete transformation of our society. God gave us this country, it is not ours to give away. Of course, the "Perpetraitors" need these vulnerable people to control in hopes that they will join them in a repudiation of our form of government. View any further illegal immigration critically and prepare to be lambasted by the Left. The immigration problems America has experienced thus far are just a shadow of what is to come if the Leftists have their way. The task before us with the current immigrants is formidable already seeing as though our manufacturing base has dwindled. Illegal Mexicans are intruding upon states such as California and Texas. We do not need to be compromising on this subject, others who waited their turn and took the citizenship test became naturalized. Theoretically, Mexico could stage an invasion of hordes of immigrants in an attempt to take back the land they lost in the Mexican War that some still believe they deserve, ironically. Texas seceded from Mexico for religious freedom from Catholicism, in part; there really are not homesteads available like when we had the immigration of the nineteenth-century, so whose property will they end up with? This is not a mysterious question; they will either rent or end up with Americans' land. Once they cross through the border, they will be competing for American jobs and labor works with supply and demand. When there is an excess of labor, wages are lower and this is one of the subjects Liberals are always trying to combat, supposedly, stagnant wages. Well, then lower the immigration. Vagrancy could become a real problem, yet again across the nation, in some places people do not even have a place to live and the "Perpetraitors" desire a free-flow of it from Mexico. Wages will not increase naturally with a continuous stream of immigrants seeking employment and the media has, undoubtedly, never pointed this out once.

These sort of beliefs do not make one a cynic, but may be held by those with much hope. The "PerpeTraitors" have no reason to be optimistic overall despite the fact that they have been able to enact certain pieces of legislation favorable to their opinions this time. America has many assailants from within and without. The public is outfitted with so many preconceptions due to the influences of the entertainment industry that Conservatives now face an uphill battle. Just look at what it did to our country after homosexuals came out on television in the late nineties as part of a concentrated agenda. Within a generation, the Supreme Court forced all states to wed them with no legal precedence. For the Left, stare decisis should only be reckoned as a crucial part of their decision making if it defends a Liberal law. The checks and balances of a separated government are challenged when the Supreme Court legislates marriages which have nothing to do with the federal government's authority. Surely, they were not interpreting the Constitution in this decision. We should have those members impeached for their extensive over-reach of power. Conservatives are better at preserving the status quo than altering the way things are, so it will be interesting to see how they propose to change whatever the Liberals have passed, which seemingly would be permanent. Citizens are more conforming to existing notions that have been adopted by the government, over time. That is how history has revealed the arrangement of opinions to be. If an opinion is a modern one that is enough of a current justification for some voters. People mistakenly believe it is the natural evolution of society to embrace new ideas while overlooking our indebtedness to the past. This "progress" has been culminating for years, where if the legislature cannot pass the agenda, the judiciary will, even if a majority of the people are against it. The extremists have deemed our flag (that we all pledge allegiance to) as a racist symbol and refuse to stand for our National Anthem. This exposition entitled the "PerpeTraitors" has thus far addressed the health-care system, the President, Antifa, the media, immigration, etc.

May it be that Trump prevails in keeping America great. With traitors at the helm of the ship-of-state, our future would be disastrous. All it takes is a small, enlightened group of people to sow the seeds of liberty and the truth shall make us to enjoy a full freedom, once again. Even if they are made to be exiles as political dissidents, God will succor them to demonstrate that tyrants may not usurp inalienable rights. What a consolation it is to recognize that no matter how crazy and full of iniquity this nation becomes the truth will go marching on. We shall be victorious over Trump's opposition in 2020, pleasing Conservatives across the country, yet again. This is an invitation to re-evaluate the Left and to recognize that they have forced the government to supersede the boundaries of the enumerated powers of the Constitution for their own popularity. These perpetraitors' inexorable opinions have led to assault in the streets of Trump supporters and they have become uncivil. They have taken over public school curriculums and now many students do not even understand

the fundamentals of knowledge which
should be a part of our educational system.
The rate at which our students are failing in
comparison to the rest of the world and in
the amount spent on each pupil is
astounding. They are no longer aware of the
dangers of an unlimited government and the
barbarities perpetuated by them throughout
history even up until modern times in a way
that is more than being merely naïve. Now it
is customary for teachers to malign our
Founders and even modern day Presidents to
weaken their patriotism which is feared
because it might lead to nationalist
sentiments.

Everywhere in this country, voters are
beginning to notice that the actions of the
government are an unfair sham. The Left
thinks that they can finally get gun control
passed now that there are all of these mass
shooting calamities. These proposals are
made by overly ambitious politicians who
think they can over-simplify an issue for the
dumbed-down citizenry. The laws on the
books about firearms are already very
burdensome. Gun-owners should get to
remain confidential considering the track
record of other governments when it comes

to their political opposition. With these new "Red Flag" laws anyone under the slightest suspicion may lose their inherent rights. These "PerpeTraitors" are downright un-American and need an unarmed populace to forward their agenda. Only a tyrant need fear his own people. A gun buy-back program is just another one of the expenses the tax and spend Liberal would try to charge the people with who as a whole do not comprehend large sums of money proportionately and the repercussions there are when it is spent. We need to be judging our decisions on what is most favorable to liberty and the people need to have the ability to alter their government by force if necessary as stated in the Declaration of Independence. We do not need people frantically relinquishing this ability and one of the Founders said that those who would sacrifice liberty for safety deserve neither of the two. Without freedom, tyrannical forces would take away one's safety, regardless, and this notion should be understood by those who study history. America has an innate inclination to be free despite the protection these perpe-traitors may offer us from ourselves. Liberty is so precious, we should not be contemplating the confiscation of AR-15s when it is more likely for a person to be struck by lightning than to be shot by one. Politicians should be willing to acknowledge all of this before being placed into office. Otherwise, they shall be considered enemies of the Bill of Rights.

These perpetraitors have no dignity, but rather arrogance and aloofness. How can the defense of abortion seem admirable to so many people when they argue that the child will not have a good life being poor? Most people throughout the entire earth's existence have been poor and some women who undergo an abortion end up being disturbed by it. How do they know what the childhood of the infant within the womb will be like based upon the present circumstances, but that is always the argument? Principalities have ruled that abortion, paradoxically, is a way of life and a right. On the other hand, it is not listed as such in any of the Bill of Rights or the Constitution, so Roe v. Wade did not interpret these documents, instead it was based upon the opinions of the Supreme Court. No one is happy about an abortion being performed, so should not this attitude reflect upon the act itself when the pregnant woman is melancholy during the situation? That is a plain observation of the facts, it would be demented to celebrate it as a joyous occasion. If it is a matter of one's own conscience, why is it completely an issue of partisanship? The heroines of the modern feminist movement are all pro-choice. At first, the feminist fought for women's suffrage, but now it's a matter of voting on giving birth, usually after a consensual act has occurred, which is not heroic. Some of these women will get an abortion based upon the father's temperament and that is a bit capricious considering that his son or daughter's death penalty thus ensues. There is really no hope for this country unless its people are willing to defy the radicals and their perpetrators of infanticide.

It is important to be able to respond adequately with our military if our country's rights or people are threatened. With that said, a standing army at peace time is pernicious to a free society if too large because they are known historically to heavily support tyrannical dictators with oppression. Restricting its size would reduce expenditures due to the fact that military spending is the largest part of our budget and to think that the government will always be trustworthy is ridiculous. When given the choice between spending on social programs or the military, it should go to the latter because this would, at least, allow Congress to follow the Constitution. Originally, military preparedness was readily provided for by the state militias, not the Army. It was unlike our National Guard in that it was made up of every able-bodied male citizen age 21-45 and the states controlled their officers. These irregular soldiers could respond in a moment's notice, long enough for an army to be raised. We would have to determine the size of the armies of England or the United States back then in proportion to their population as to what was considered too large in order to realize what should be the correct size of today's military. The political divide is stronger than it used to be and the Democrats are known as being weak on the military and foreign policy. It is almost a mystery as to why they cannot be on the right side of anything, for the one thing that is most important for the Federal government to operate is a functional military.

Rejecting the radicals' agenda that sounds like the Sirens sweetly singing requires thorough contemplation; Marxists are behind much of the Left's political agenda including centralizing in Federal agencies all aspects of society. Robin Hood was infamous for stealing from the rich to give to the poor, but what is not said by these Perpetraitors usually was why England was so poor; it was because of taxes. In his day, there was no upward mobility and wealth was ancestral. This type of inherited wealth is now the target of dissatisfaction, mainly because of the fictional books and movies of the last century. Notice how a common theme is always the poor man who tried to change or upset the hierarchy or who stood up to money. Now how could this not be viewed as persuasive and it is all juxtaposed with soul-killing sex scenes? Or else, the motif is constantly challenging the status quo and social mores until they become acceptable as though society is thought to be gaining something from it. In these films and literature, the audience is introduced to all sorts of new ideas that are meant to change peoples' opinions and unknowingly do. Many times parts that appear ambiguous have an ulterior motive and are merely another arm of the Communist propaganda machine that is necessary to them to garner support in a democracy. Comrades, let us glory the proletariat, there is no God, say the "PerpeTraitors". Anything paternal must be challenged at a young age because that is where the idea of authority stems psychologically from until the government takes over every aspect of one's life to replace it. Deliverance from one's life and responsibilities may only come through revolution, says the Marxist, once one's life becomes unbearable under a mere quasi-Capitalist system freshly adapted for revolutionary tendencies. The Socialist groups know that their policies regress eventually into Communism which should be viewed as perdition.

Chapter III

In addition, the Republicans are accusing the Democrats of holding a Soviet-style impeachment inquiry. Impeachment is like a Grand Jury indictment by the House of Representatives and amounts to little more than a public censure if two-thirds of the Senate do not convict. Since the President's

party controls it, he will not be removed
from office despite that being the
Democrats' obsession. Only two other
Presidents have been impeached by their
enemies: Andrew Johnson and Bill Clinton
for perjury and obstruction of justice. If
Donald Trump faces this misfortune, too,
nothing will change politically. In fact,
because the establishment is so
enthusiastically against him, people will
begin to count that as a sign that he is on the
right track as far as breaking down the
corruption of the Deep State operatives.
Trump is what is considered a populist
leader which means he champions the
opinions of the common man. He is
positioned to win his re-election like many
incumbents, having raised 125 million
dollars in campaign funds in one quarter
alone. Everything he does is controversial to
the Leftists, but his agenda has been
formulated by common sense. Even though
Putin was a member of the KGB, Russia is
no longer Communist, but the Democrats
are still trying to drudge up old resentments
between the nations in order to raise the
opposition against our President. Ironically,
the GOP has been the most outspoken
against the USSR and now that they are free,

it is the Democrats who are complaining about them. The public should see the hypocrisy of the perpe-traitors and how unexpected it is to see the tables turned on Russia by the Left, once they are no longer Communists bent on world conquest.

These petty, scrupulous accusations against the Commander-in-Chief are backed by the media who want more viewers for their advertisers. It is nothing odd that the media has been like this since its beginning centuries ago and has always solicited change. If one wishes to forfeit one's rights, he should follow these perpetraitors who are shutting down communications on the internet and banning individuals from platforms. No free Republic can withstand this perpetually because it is up to the people to preserve their way of life and they are being silenced. This is called massive manipulation to force more government control over our lives. Every economic recession we have had since the late fifties has resulted in a loss of factories and they have not been coming back from overseas. This slippage from the leading industrial economy to an almost purely service economy is being touted by the educational establishment as evolutionary progress because they have not even considered taking on the banks that control the growing debts of hundreds of millions of people. A strategic approach to our National Debt would include more production of exports and this is exactly what the President's tariffs are doing. Our artificial employment rates do not include everyone who could potentially work, so as not to cause alarm. In order for America to be successful, more people need to depend on work for their livelihood. This has been misrepresented by the media. The real facts are unavailable, once they are able to be exposed. People are acting like freedom is a privilege and not a God-given right these days and the public educational system is partly to blame. People need to be able to express love and emotion, not just the gift of knowledge, but instead the television and seven hours of silence in the classroom are producing automatons just like the perpe-traitors desire. These are the consequences of that sort of lifestyle: acclimation to a prisoner mentality, perversion, criminal behavior, and deviant immorality. It is no wonder people tried to free their minds, but from all the wrong things were they persuaded to do so in these educational facilities where prayer is banned. The television possesses such prominence in most homes and that is life's alternative to slaving because of debt or secular schooling. It has become popular to spew forth profanity and sarcasm; to practice insubordination, fornication, and substance abuse; and to speak evil of others, all as a reaction. People have become unaccustomed to righteousness.

We are facing financial doom if this chaos continues unabated. Overshadowing everything said thus far is America's problems concerning the Christian faith. The majority of the next generation no longer has any faith whatsoever and this was primarily the goal of the Communists. Migration to the colonies for religious reasons was what started this great nation. Now we are in a religious crisis where a large number of people have categorized religious expression as "hate speech", especially when pertaining to sin. Our heritage is in Christianity as a country. The perpetraitors want us groveling to them for sustenance. They want us paralyzed in fear of the government. Satan was the conqueror in the Bolshevik Revolution, no other, and we are still suffering as a planet in the aftermath of that catastrophe. Christians are the enemy to the schemes of the perpetraitors because they know that we will practice civil disobedience when compelled to do so by our God. Only, the church has become another instrument of Liberalism in our modern era. They have fundamentally sought to alter our religion with higher criticism and nonliteral interpretations of the Bible. The concentration of the opposition is across the board. People seldom notice the ramifications of what is being taught in our schools these days from sex education to evolution. These perpetraitors are becoming more aggressive for what they call social justice where we must support reparations and transgender tolerance, etc. Eventually, they will use cruelty to enforce their opinions. There was already a transgender attack on a man preaching the Bible in public; he ended up bloody while the assailant eluded the authorities. This all originated in the Communist agenda which suggested homosexuality should be normalized in America to weaken our people. Notice how there is no outrage over a gay man running for President, now. We have been living in the Apocalypse it seems.

There are a lot of events that have indicated this. This publication will try to steer away from eschatology as much as possible, as if it could get any more controversial.

In order to get away with their crimes against the state, these perpe-traitors have become master deceivers. These people are inwardly scoundrels of the basest sort and upon all reflection make themselves to appear seemingly benevolent. They would have you believe that a national utopia of the brotherhood of man is progress, asserting peace when there is no peace. What this country needs are leaders that are immovable to compromise with the Left because they have learned to ask for much more so that the agreement will begin at their actual goals. Concessions to the enemy must only be made when we are desperate. In lieu of what Americans deserve, we have settled for less than what the perpe-traitors proposed allowing them to gradually grow the government with burdensome regulations, new costly programs, etc. Make no mistake, our side triumphs without political bargaining, not the other way around. This country must be preserved by re-enforcing the Constitutional limits on the

Federal government. We do not need omniscience when it comes to testing more government spending on programs; we already know what will occur if they are initiated. The proposition on the part of Conservatives is a restoration of the limited government of our Constitutional Republic in accordance to the will of our Founders who feared oppression. We must preserve the inheritance of our ancestors, not cede the land to immigrants who already outnumber naturally born citizens in some areas. We have already settled for assurances that the legislation passed by the Left will not slide us down "the slippery slope" and yet time and again it turns against us. We cannot afford a continuance of the march of so called progress, when this "progress" leads to the abolition of private property in the means of production like a significant segment of the next generation agrees with. Make no mistake, first governments subjugate property owners and then the commoners' subjugation soon follows.

It has begun with the Inquisition of Brett Kavanaugh and Donald Trump, but the foundations have already been laid through the questions courts may ask the "mentally ill" who own firearms or who have children like, "Do you ever feel angry? Are you against the government?" They have already weeded out and labeled a quarter of our population with professionals who will be trained as thought police who have also anathematized anyone who believes their religion is the best or is intolerant of others. The Left is striving for an amalgamation of all of the people in the world here in America believing that the existence of races cause war, but just as God dispersed those at the Tower of Babel who thought they could do anything once joined together, this effort is doomed to failure. There are passions from both sides of the aisle who have recognized that we are to treat strangers as we should like to be treated and by this biblical term is meant those of another race who live amongst us. Christendom has always been like this. A sentimentalist believes in this wholeheartedly, but this seems like the only lesson that is taught these days by the establishment and it may have shifted to the forefront for solely pragmatic reasons of self-preservation and to avoid law-suits. No one can deny that Karl Marx was an advocate of this, as well, because he preached that property could not be re-distributed unless all races banded together in order for that purpose to be profitable to the masses. He alleged that racism was merely a tool of the Capitalists to divide and conquer the people; he began to conceive the notion of class envy, as well. The only thing is these are not peaceful beliefs he has contrived because he knew that Communism could not be successful as long as there were Capitalist states outside of this sphere: these were to be occupied through invasion or revolutionary insurgents. Once the Communists take-over a country, there is bloody retribution for anyone in the upper classes who would defy them, the land is raided, and ruthlessly pillaged. The results would be tumultuous for our inhabitants.

God bestows upon us great virtue. We have always appreciated education as a people and the cultivation of one's intellect. We have faced many hardships and still the people perish for lack of knowledge. Our soldiers have been indefatigable in their defense of freedom when challenged by evil. Americans are of a friendly disposition, but staunch defenders of their natural rights. The despicable perpe-traitors have betrayed the trust of the American people, taking advantage of their naïve reliance on usury through cupidity. The alienations that have occurred because of them are ungodly and all of the preceding transfer of property to the banking conglomerates from the people should be rightfully returned. The sheering of the property of the common man is imprudent and has created a vast concentration of wealth in the hands of sinners. This would be true justice, under God. The right to be secure in one's property is ancient and the Communists have sought to do away with it altogether. This country will never cease to exist, but the dissolution of what it once was has been nearly completed by the perpe-traitors. The immediate restitution of all of the farmers' property and other land-owners' properties taken before 1970 is now in order. It is only fair that the banking cartel gets to keep it for fifty years and no more or else our children will lose their inheritances becoming homeless, strangled by debt as Jefferson warned as a consequence. The preliminaries of this action will include the forming of a committee in Congress designated to restoring the property fairly according to legal documentation and shall be disinterested in the banks' corporate lobbying. No one owns these institutions any longer anyways; they have become an abstract tool of Satan, leeching off of the good, productive people and a scourge to our economy.

All liberty-loving individuals need to band together and oust these perpe-traitors. They are already persuading people to look upon our Constitution contemptuously, calling it outdated because they disagree with it. They hope to circumvent aspects of it, like the Electoral College, without even passing an amendment which is the only lawful procedure for changing this potent document which is the basis of our government. One way to be more successful is to form a companionship with a like - minded individual. Make a decision to donate to a Conservative's campaign or join organizations that seek to preserve the heritage of our people. One's local Tea Party is always welcoming for patriots who wish to yet again shed the yoke of tyranny and taxation. If one will associate with others through freedom of assembly, it can persuade opportunist politicians to change their tune. The truth is on our side, so the more these issues are talked about, the more votes wholesome candidates will receive, so do not get discouraged. That is why they are trying to make it rude to talk about politics, but that is one hundred percent American and keeps people from being confused by the media. The perpe-traitors would make political speech rare, if possible, so that the voters are forced to rely on Liberal mouth-pieces. These politicians who vote for more taxes, pensions, and subsidies for their government workers are like thieves. Their pleas for fleecing the flock are accentuated by the propaganda in pop-culture, aforementioned. Their views are radical and used to indoctrinate our nation's youth. Corrupting the younger generation that lacks wisdom inevitably will lead to this country's ruin. In the secular environment of the classroom these ideas inculcated in students go unchallenged, but be reluctant to warn them of any of this or they will turn against you or report what you say. Recruiting them to the right-side can be done by others eventually after they have an opportunity to begin living their lives after schooling. The teachers are already molding them into their own party; they are overwhelmingly Democrat because of the unions. They no longer teach the spirit of patriotism in our public schools like they once did. It is politically expedient for them to have lengthened the amount of time our children are educated with Head Start and, of course, there might be free college brainwashing for all. With the youngest generation there is now a constant struggle to get them to maintain a basic belief system of love to one's country and the concept of universal truth.

If we still would like to continue being the wealthiest nation, we must possess superiority in the manufacturing sector or our riches will wane. The price of liberty is eternal vigilance, so we are to watch and pray. The latest trend is to label news from Conservative sources as conspiracy theories, so beware. We have to get men elected who will pledge to a balanced budget. Once they have maintained a decent voting record of low spending, they may be re-elected. Trillions of dollars in national debt will cause us to lapse into another depression. Their verbal commitments to reducing expenditures and paying portions of the debt, which was the practice of our legislators for our country's first seventy-five years, must be unfeigned. These Leftists who are squeezing the life out of the country are guilty of perpetrating the greatest scheme ever concocted to overthrow a government from within. Some of them are now claiming that unless we spend trillions more and stifle industry, the planet will face irreversible devastation and all mankind will perish in twenty years. No, our country will end because of debt and due to these affronts to common sense. This is a reminder to never vote for anyone who will raise your own taxes. I would hate to see us try to fight a war right now, usually debts are caused by them, but not this time. One aspect of the Civil War's victory was that the Southern enemy was broke and had less men. Be warned, China outnumbers us and we are borrowing money from them to finance our government. We are overburdened with debt and taxation. Our children will be forced to pay interest to Communists because of our insolence, indolence, and unfunded government liabilities. Our only hope is that we refuse to surrender our weapons, en masse, to the police when they turn on the people. The Leftists are shrewd and have anticipated that we would be uncooperative, so the confiscation of firearms is happening gradually. We do not want to face the fury of an invasion unarmed, but the criminal elements are forcing our leaders into making the wrong decisions. More evidence of a possible threat is the effeminacy of our countrymen. It certainly is not an improvement in our defense! We need men who are brave to keep this country from being conquered, not cowards. Chivalric protectors of our innate rights are necessary for survival. We need men who have been raised with discipline and who are accustomed to shooting guns. This would further distinguish us from other countries who have largely outlawed firearms, making us stronger and hardy. Otherwise, we might scarcely be able to put down Communist insurrections or a foreign attack. We cannot go back to the pioneer days, but we can still keep the spirit of rugged individualism that was necessary to settle this vast territory. America has earned world renown and has the distinction of being the first grand Republic of the modern era, so it would be a shame if this great experiment failed and if America should no longer be prosperous. Right now, the parties are beginning to be at enmity with one another. It is difficult for them to accomplish any sort of legislation and that is a good thing considering that most of it has been bad. The intensity for the support and opposition for a President has gotten high with Donald Trump. The amount of debt has been unsurpassed and each side is blaming the other with the Democrats accusing the Republicans of too much military spending and tax cuts to increase it, while the Democrats are guilty of trying to raise spending on everything else and taxes. Neither side is viewed as being favorable to most Americans for the government is constantly expanding with more taxes. Regardless, the bias of the media is in favor of an unlimited government. Our leaders today are not very pithy and seem disingenuous especially now that they speak with microphones and tele-prompters. Also, much of the public is oblivious to politics and voter participation has been low for the most part, especially in the primaries. People have lost all patience for politics because of all of the broken promises.

Chapter IV

The Socialists are redistributionists of wealth through taxation, for one example. Still they have captured the minds of the next generation, who, according to the polls, are the age group that has the highest support for Socialism. I think there is, at least, a two-fold explanation for this: the inadequacy of the educational system in condemning it and the inadequacy of the jobs available due to widespread decline in manufacturing. Yet, the voice of the American people is against big-government Socialism. The prevailing opinion in most parts of the country is still for Donald Trump. It would be a major disappointment if he was not re-elected. Identifying these perpe-traitors is not that difficult because they seem to lie most frequently with the Democratic Party or else they will be outspoken against the President. So discovering them should be easy, they are for globalism and change always. The Democrats, as said before, have become considerably more Left-wing. These monsters are now saying that if a fetus is born viable, but was supposed to be aborted, it can still be aborted after it is born. It is a tragedy that they have been able to convince the youth that abortion is a moral option to pregnancy, ensuring that no child will suffer from inferior circumstances in this dystopia. Our people face damnation because of abortion and all the Left can do is claim its opponents are anti-women when half of the aborted babies would grow up to be women. Support for abortion has actually become popular now that it is government sanctioned. The same type of people who were supporters of eugenics in the early-twentieth century are probably now for the euthanasia of Alzheimer's patients, so that they can avoid suffering. These executioners will go to hell for taking God's life into their own hands. Abortion is the number one problem our country has and only gun control comes second. Both are terrible laws concocted by those who would side with dictators on many issues.

Although the freedom of speech is usually associated with protest, the next generation no longer believes that "hate speech" (to use Newspeak) should be protected by the First Amendment. Two young men were recently prosecuted in Connecticut for using the word nigger when it was not even being directed at anyone; however backward the usage of the term is, we have a right to decide whether or not to say anything. How could anything be so convolutedly authoritarian? Some Southerners still use that word somewhat frequently because they hold grudges against the North for emancipating their slaves in order to shoot at the Southerners. Sure their language is filled with contempt, but it should not be a crime. Less people are using the word these days and it was almost reserved to people of old age a while ago, so now this oppression is rearing its ugly head. The Founders knew that a majority-rule system would endanger the rights of those outside of the majority, so they left safeguards against it in our Constitution and Bill of Rights because they abominated tyranny. Most people would not desire a totalitarian government that is the antithesis of freedom. Regretfully, this is the way most people in authority are led to believe they should be handling things because of political correctness. It makes people nervous and many people who are very tolerant are critical of how much political correctness has expanded to include things unheard of in the Baby-Boom generation. This is yet another restriction upon our inalienable rights. These perpe-traitors want us begging for leniency over statements, now, or we will face fines and imprisonment.

Another tyrannical act has been the confiscation of gold from U.S. citizens under FDR. Just think of the arrogance of this man to do so and to have also attempted to add members to the Supreme Court for striking down his programs that were faithfully ruled un-Constitutional. Now the presumptuous Left has brainwashed most to believe that this man saved us from the Depression with his extra government spending when in reality it was the war that did so. This is the dogma of the perpe-traitors. There is no appreciation for the actions of the United States unless it relates to Federal programs with them. There are literally revisionists of our own history. They have transmitted lies for a century to conform to their own political bias. Now there is even apostasy in the main-line Protestant denominations. They still adhere to monotheism, but they are neglective in supporting the literal Word of God if it is not politically correct. Since when did the clergy become rebellious of the Bible, this happened after the "Communist Manifesto" was published? This is when the

secularization of our institutions began, as
well. One of the goals of Marxism is to
annihilate Christianity because it stands in
the way of revolutions and totalitarian
government. One of the criterion for being a
Communist is an adherence to atheism. It is
like a prerequisite for these Perpe-traitors, as
well. None will acknowledge our Christian
heritage publicly, but may mention God
once or twice in an hour-long speech. There
are no exhortations from these demagogues.
They should be made to confess before a
judge that they have betrayed the
Constitution. Their actions have stretched
the "necessary and proper" clause beyond its
limits. The perpetraitors have acted foolishly
and recklessly in expanding the government
past the boundaries our Founders put in
place for it. If they were faithful in
executing the duties of their office, we
would not have gotten into trillions of
dollars of debt during small wars in the
Middle East. Needless to say, most would
agree that our spending needs improvement.
If we would like our children's children to
experience freedom, we cannot keep going
on the path we have taken. Our soldiers have
been glorious in victory for the liberty of the
people. They are ready to preserve our

freedom at a moment's notice with their own blood. They have marched forward beneath our wondrous flag and Leftists are refusing to rise for our National Anthem.

Our people must be willing to stand up in the face of adversity and rebuke wickedness. What happens if our country faces hardship; we have nothing saved away for a rainy day? The expense of our government is already exceedingly great which has been stated here on numerous occasions. The ship of state has become submerged. We must prevent it from becoming permanently sunk in the abysmal waters of debt. It is high time for the fraternities across this promised-land to realize this and band together, presenting new leadership. These organizations instill confidence in our nation's youth and prevent men from becoming anti-social. Politics is a social aspect of government and fraternities allied will provide the necessary strength to remain obstinate to any new spending initiatives. They already have in place a structural network of communication that will be handy in gaining a mastery in political influence. We also need coherent arguments presented to members who sometimes are brain-washed by the Liberal establishment. The infringement upon States' rights are insufferable, given that our Ninth and Tenth Amendments ensure these liberties as does the Constitution with its enumerated powers. Dissensions have arisen on campuses lately when Conservatives attempt to exercise their freedom of speech to where the President has had to step-in and demand that this right is protected or else the colleges will lose their Federal funding. Many times the Conservatives are accused of being bigots which is an ongoing tactic of the Left to smear their credibility. Fraternities are also becoming targets because they are masculine, predominantly white, and well-to-do compared to welfare recipients. In order to penetrate this potential opposition perpetraitors of the Left are beginning to advocate the destruction of all male fraternities as being sexist. Fraternities have marvelous property across America, but this effort by extremists to abridge their right to peaceably assemble reflects the totalitarian views of the Left. Fraternities could be a platform of traditionalism, therefore they are a threat to the PerpeTraitors. They give young men a chance to bond and who knows what they will talk about? The perpetraitors see danger in fraternal relationships because they are away from the media and thought police professors and could perhaps lead to an individual becoming critical of the establishment. Young men might gradually be drifting away from the "newspeak", per se. Once Communists take-over, they focus on the eradication of such possible forums of dissent. They have the ability to be persistent in their demands and there is probably, at least, a million men alive today who have been in a fraternity. Conservative opposition does not spontaneously arise like the Left that spawns riots, but is well organized beforehand. It is imperative that we take possession of Congress and the State governments. These perpetraitors are guilty of incivility and there are at least one hundred cases of this against Trump supporters.

Trump has done well for the War on Terror by instating a "travel ban" from countries where terrorists are in operation. It was almost futile for the Left to object that it was in reality a Muslim ban because the courts upheld it. They tried to play the "race card" on Trump in this situation, like many others, and it did not work. His mentality is to do the right thing and to not cower before political and potential accusations. The attacks on him from the Left have been unparalleled and this is perhaps because he has sided with an outnumbered ideologically Conservative faction that is against illegal immigration. We have not had a focus on controlling immigration properly since like the Coolidge Administration. We do not need idle immigrants to weigh down our Socialistic programs that are used to sabotage our country that is why the President is proposing that immigrants should be required to show that they can pay for their own health-care. Once this has been arranged, we can let them in because they will not be a burden on our government. Some people in the interior of the country do not realize that Mexicans are now more prevalent in American states bordering Mexico than the original stock of people who settled this country. This is due to the carelessness of past Presidents who have not seen to it that our laws are faithfully executed. When illegal aliens have violated the law by not applying for citizenship, they have been granted blanket amnesty by the millions. Universal amnesty schemes like DACA are most likely illegal. One will not see many who espouse Conservatism among the perpe-traitors of this country's demise. Many Liberals wish that the President would be assassinated which demonstrates their evil world-view.

The Republicans have aided our economy through major "trickle-down" tax-cuts, tariffs, and ending costly regulations. When the government bureaucracy subjects businesses to constant inspection with thousands of regulations devised by un-elected officials, those businesses have to hire someone expensive to sit and read all of them and possess lawyers to avoid excessive fines that are un-Constitutional. Even after paying out all of this money which cuts into profits, to comply with the over burdensome regulations in court, the verdict reached may still be against them. We cannot afford to have these ambitious Leftists against Capitalism destroying industry. The responsibility should rest on patriotic Americans who are pro-business. People who are for our system and do not view everything as exploitation of the worker are needed if businesses are to compete on a global scale. The Industrial Revolution made laborers more numerous and helped to increase efficiency in the manufacture of products and spread the wealth to others besides the aristocratic land-owners. The Left views the old, peasant agrarian system negatively, the industrial age as the bane of mankind especially environmentally, and is against how things are today, so in spite of our prosperity all they will ever do is spawn discontent. Providence has ordained the natural system of property and wages throughout the history of mankind and mere men should not be "playing God" with the economy with a Communist system. When people see the word Socialism these days, there is a misapprehension because they do not see how it tends to develop into Communism. Many millions have been terminated under these regimes because once liberty is suppressed there is no longer any means for resistance. Unfortunately, Communists have infiltrated our institutions beginning under FDR and there has been a gradual rise in the redistribution of wealth, subsequently. Their government has continued to grow unrestrained and now even Social Security is scheduled to become insolvent in the near future. It is important to get to know your State representative, if he is a Republican, so you can voice your opinion personally. All hope is lost with the Democrats who are obsessed with appearing benevolent at every opportunity instead of demonstrating fiscal responsibility.

The people have become slowly acclimated to this Welfare-State. The poor's reliance on the government is astounding; it used to be that the local governments and churches would support the indigent population. This would be a much needed reform because the way things have turned out with our Federal government has been a total disappointment. Right now with it overstepping its functions past the limits of our Constitution, its authority has become arbitrary. England has been going the same way ever since the Labour Party came into being arguing for Socialism. One can see how both have become decadent. Just think of all of the fraud that goes on with Federal excess. We are entangled with every abominable nation known to man, as well, through endless treaties. Today Republicans are talking about preventing a Socialist take-over in our country, but this nation has been slowly transformed into that already. This is to the consternation of all patriots and the last chance we had for one to take office

before most of it took place was Barry
Goldwater. The hand-outs increase
incessantly because the people are not
responsible enough to vote against them.
Our form of government has not failed, the
politicians have failed in its preservation. It
has existed precariously for at least a
century and the Socialists running for
President are about to be our death knell. A
politician actually just proposed a
preposterous 93 trillion dollar deal to save
the environment and all of the highest
potential tax schemes are not even able to
pay for it! Hard-work and achievement are
no longer to be sought after, now that food is
free for the poor, also. The demands of the
Left have become intolerable. They will
scare people into thinking there will be mass
starvation without the Federal government,
but historically this is not true and the
individual States possess the sole authority
under our Bill of Rights to provide food for
the needy. Again, notice how the cities were
the only areas to vote Democrat in the
Presidential Election and they have become
unruly with crime. The cities are distressed
and full of Leftists. The eruption of violence
in the gun control zones demonstrates that it
will not work and it is no wonder that the

Bible says to flee the cities in the last days. The city council and mayor of Chicago are considering providing a basic income to residents and if this is not Communist, nothing is. The inevitable outcome of the Leftist media and teachers is Socialism if the people will not restrain themselves. Americans used to view themselves as being superior to the rest of the world, but the Left teaches nothing but shame. The politicians will not even speak about the fundamentals of our Constitution because the interpretations have become so broad.

Trump ran on restoring the United States to its former grandeur, his "Make America Great Again" campaign. The music was even better back then instead of all of this insane garbage put out these days, which is a reflection upon our society then and now. People would have called you crazy if you owned an Asian-made automobile. The Left could not find anything but approbation for Trump as though he was using the slogan to campaign for slavery. Now with confidence in how his administration has turned things around, President Trump would like to "Keep America Great". Back then, most marriages did not end in a divorce and most infants were not born out of wed-lock; this country had virtue. That is not to say divorce is evil, but these facts certainly show that the circumstances are currently unfavorable. Also, a large portion of the younger generation, after reaching maturity, are not leaving home and the average age to get married is approaching thirty. Recent history, to them, has faded into obscurity and unfortunately all they may have been told is that America was never great. The Perpe-traitors' whole harangue would be about taking peoples' money away involuntarily and giving it away to those who have not earned it in an income redistribution scheme. It would be nothing about how we have won every major war in perilous times except maybe Vietnam. The deceptive masks these men have worn ever since the advent of Communism are satanic. They have been tenacious against the word empire which the Communists preached about, trying to label America as one. They have been rudimentarily opposed to the British Empire who were practically our cousins, for the same purpose, their hidden Communist agenda. This is all in the name of progress as the empires collapsed, the African countries fell to Communism or

Muslim radical dictators. These Communists
have determination and will fight to the
death to overthrow our government like they
did in Vietnam and Korea. Their history of
ruling countries is unscrupulous, at best. In
order for an act passed by our government to
be legitimate, it must also be Constitutional,
but now our Supreme Court has become the
final voice on this issue with little credibility
after interpreting it in Roe v. Wade and gay
marriage. Another result of these perpetraitors has been the dramatic decrease in
tithes received by the churches because of
high taxes and more recently because of
rampant disbelief. It seems like the majority
of Christian correspondence meant for
unbelievers is done apologetically as though
an acceptance of religious intellectual
arguments has the power to save one's soul.
Also, you will find that almost half of the
faculty at any given secular educational
institution of higher learning are atheist. It is
an atrocity that Christianity is not taught in
our schools, but that is because of the failure
of the Supreme Court. All of the social and
criminal problems increased once prayer
was removed from schools, detracting from
their authority. This would have been
intolerable to our nation's Founders who

knew that the freedom to exercise religion is
unalienable. A separation of church and
state is nowhere in our Constitution, the
government was just prohibited from
declaring any one Christian sect the state
religion. They had nothing against Jesus.
The Constitution was not about the
elimination of religion. Now our children
are surrendered against our will to atheists
only to return home to a television that is
secular, as well. The moral fabric of our
society has been deteriorating ever since.

Chapter V

Not only that, we are losing our American
work ethic. America is known for its
resilience, coming back from the
devastations of the Revolutionary and Civil
Wars on her own soil, many other wars, and
the World Wars. We do not retreat from our
duties, but ensure that the people of the earth
are blessed through us. We lead the world in
technology thanks to our patent office
instituted by the U.S. Constitution. The
United States has historically received a
high literacy rate thanks to its dedication to
education and people from all over the

world come to study at our universities. She is known for her liberties. Now these distinctions have become blurred by the objections of the Left who view everything in light of global equality. The Communist goal is the neutralizing of America from within and without. Another one of their goals was to take over one or more of the political parties in the United States and within my own lifetime all of the social Conservatives have left the Democratic Party and it has totally been in favor of "big government". They used to be for tariffs, too, and thank God Trump has re-instituted them, so that the malevolent Chinese cannot profit off of America, with their oppression and forced abortions. Vietnam was a war against Communists like the Chinese which was fought to liberate the people and prevent the evil from spreading across the globe. Other poverty-ridden countries have fallen for the false promises of the authoritarian world-view. There were Soviet sympathizers found within the Deep State before World War II even, but now we are taught by these same sympathizers to laugh this off as just being the "Red Scare". The beliefs of McCarthyism really were not a myth, though. Understanding these perpetraitors' intentions is the key to interpreting the developments of the last century. They have been a hindrance to our government, economy, and institutions ever since their infiltration. There has been much corroboration of the evidence that will attest to this fact. We have received no intermission from their continual assault on American values. People speak with hesitation about this for fear of being viewed as a conspiracy theorist because the establishment does not preach it. One of the goals of the Communist Party was to take over the media and educational establishment, so this opinion should be considered conspicuous. The way in which they have had to stealthily impose their agenda because it would not be adopted forthright reflects negatively upon it.

This should not be a revelation to anyone, but to all Americans this should be well known. Communists bemoan labor that merely rewards one's subsistence, but then turn around and hypocritically condone a total dependence on a centralized government by someone with zero productivity. To think this is somehow fairer and honorable is demented. These perpetraitors want a one-world government where all sovereign nations are ended. These elites who would have rule over us look at everyone else in an aloof way as though we are ignorant, that our ideas such as patriotism cause war. The Soviet Union was hell-bent on world conquest, but checked by the United States. Any autonomous state is even a threat to their plans and anyone who would seek to rule the world would be considered a madman, if not the Anti-Christ. Internationalists or globalists always claim that anything against their schemes is isolationist which they have coined as a negative term, but these same people bemoan the United States' departure from this policy as imperial. Why this inherent contradiction exists is because they no longer possess a loyalty to our country. After the American Revolution was fought for our independence from Great Britain, why would we submit to a rule from an international government? This predicted one-world government would view any opposition to mass immigration as discrimination. Capitalists would presumably become a target under this regime. Allegiance to a global Communist ideology will pervade every institution of higher learning across the world. This international hegemony will come to power amidst wars and rumors of wars when the people will chant for peace when there is none. The propensities of the international proletariat will have the appearance of godliness, tamed by the entertainment industry with desensitizing fear and violence, while denying the power thereof. The banking system will become more prosperous than ever. Any remnant of privilege that defies the New World Order, like the ancient aristocracy, will be murdered just like in Russia and France. These perpe-traitors will be setting up a dictatorship under the guise of a one world religion that will be more than a mere confederacy. This enormous abomination will be a revival of the Holy Roman Empire, the same one Napoleon tried to re-create and Hitler attempted to resurrect. The masses will be deluded into thinking that this is for their benefit and safety. The world will be filled with injustice and the lusts of mankind will be insatiable. People will be hypnotized by wall-screens and placed under a delusion to report each other for any hint of disloyalty to the Beast. The merchants shall wax great in abundance. The inalienable rights of man shall be no more. Anyone for their old countries or traditional religion shall be deemed a miserable racist and the Great Whore of the economy, which may come to be signified as usury, shall become drunk with the blood of their martyrdom. Everyone will be tranquilized as though it is their civic duty to be on psychotropic medication. Of course, proliferating this international allegiance will be a spiritual "Mark of the Beast" which no one may buy, sell, or trade without. Those who resist will be rich Christians who bought gold ahead of time and use servantry for exchanges in lieu of having to receive the mark, but they will be severely persecuted. The world will become such an amalgamation due to miscegenation that only 144,000 of God's chosen people will be left of the original stock who have not died under the strength of oppression. Also, an epidemic of abortion and homosexuality will decrease their population to that number. One will be guilty of nonconformity if one does not abstain from marriage and procreates. Few will fight back; look what happened to the whole continent of Indians even though they did resist. The Novus Ordo Seclorum will tout the responsibilities we have to our environment and will have a goal to reduce the population by billions just like the United Nations agenda. Once the perpe-traitors force this to start happening, no one will escape the wars, famines, pestilences, etc. This is not unimaginable for it has been foreseen in the Book of Revelation. There will be harassment by world police with no methods for a redress of grievances. The one world government will not be very picturesque, to say the least.

These perpe-traitors are extremely methodical. They have gradually taken over all of the facets of our government. CNN especially demonstrates contempt for our President and this would have even been the case had he not have picked a fight with this network, specifically. Its news pundits are predominantly Liberal and have yet to provide a fair and balanced approach to news-casting. When they are against Conservatism, it is no longer the subtle brain-washing of yesteryear, they are emphatic. Any discrepancy with the narrative, agenda, or talking-points of the Left is quickly disregarded and swept under the rug. For instance, the narrative is that Mr. Trump is particularly cruel against immigrants, when in reality the Obama Administration did the same thing and deported even more illegals than Trump's. The Conservatives gave into a stupendous concession while nominating Trump who is tolerant of homosexuals, but this compromise was still not good enough for the Left. That was essentially the most divisive social issue of our time and the Republican President more or less conceded it to the Liberals by no longer challenging gay marriage. The perpe-traitors have been busy obliterating the family unit for decades to weaken the populace who could have possibly formed a resistance to the coming evil. The Left does not refer to the Nazi as Socialist although the word was in the name of their party because they try to group them with the Right-wing. When compared and contrasted the similarities with the Nazis to the Right-wing are broad, whereas their affinity to the Left is more specific. A broad comparison can be made, for example, that some Conservatives are racist and so were Nazis, but this book was not written to vindicate either. The Left acts like the Communists are unsullied in comparison to the Nazis because they did not go after the Jews, but the Soviets murdered tens of millions of more Christians that the Nazis did Jews. This fact goes against the historical narrative that the Left uses to portray Christianity as the oppressor. If the Left was properly associated with these Communist perpe-traitors, like this book draws a connection between, it would revolutionize public opinion against them. The American public now knows little about Bolshevism in comparison to the Nazis. The promulgation of the effects of the "Communist Manifesto" is necessary in preventing its doctrine from taking hold in America. People need to be informed of the dangers of big government immediately, before the PerepTraitors win. Perhaps the author should establish the following directly: the perpetraitors, the Left, Socialists, Liberals, and Communists are all associated with one another in this book. We shall be fortunate to avoid the influences of any of them in this country, but it should be stated that the Liberal may be ignorant of the effects of his policies when being equated to the Communist. It is enough that each seek to disarm their political opponents with far reaching gun control that will eventually lead to confiscation. That should be a good enough elucidation of what patriots are up against. Gun control is being modified by Red Flag laws now so that hearsay can determine an individual's worthiness to bear arms, but the Left will have to find a way to keep their own weapons if they are to support the anarchy of a Communist Antifa revolution. Therefore, there will probably be some sort of favoritism that develops where "racists" are not allowed to own guns due to their potential threat, but this is uncertain. Remember the unworthy quest to label Mr. Trump and all his supporters as racists and one may get the picture. The fulfillment of this prediction shan't take long now that there is hate crime legislation and Red Flag laws. Having bigoted views about anything will get one fired now in a deliberate effort to control one's freedom of thought, speech, expression, etc. It is up to the reader to decide whether or not this is a new blessing upon America. I guess this is an attempt to eradicate the last vestiges of racism in our country, only the problem is not nearly as prevalent as it used to be.

Be prepared for mass confusion, once the perpe-traitors make their final move. There will be lots of Americans who are vehemently opposed to Socialism who will

be accused of turning a blind eye towards
those who are in need of health-care. Once
the poor get a taste of Socialism, they will
be forced to forfeit their privacy and the
Federal government will have a dossier on
everyone. The Right-wing is being
reasonable when it comes to Communists,
for the most part, is allowing them their
free-speech, and not convicting them of
treason. Communists have not taken an
active role, prominently, in the Democratic
Party, but have rather supported the agenda
behind the scenes. That is why the party did
not initially face the indignation of the
people because they were busy on shifting
the opinions of our nation's youth through
text books, etc. The resemblance between
Socialism and Communism is no
coincidence and often it is the Communists
who are orchestrating the support for the
Socialist legislation. The basis for all
gradualistic Communist take-overs would be
Socialism. There would be more opportunity
in this country, if it were not for the
Socialistic programs that hamper economic
growth. Though, that is like the deal we
have now; it is like offering a vampire some
blood so as not to be killed, at first. It is
already a given that people will have an

impulse towards free things from the government, until they are educated about true fairness. These Leftists are the same ones who held our Vietnam veterans in contempt and spit in their faces. They are always generous with other people's money, aka., the taxpayer, when they are in support of legislations. One wonders how our country has been sustained for this long with blatant violations to our Constitution that also protects them from being prosecuted for treason, due to its strict definition in the document. They seek for the people, salvation through the government, as though Washington, D.C. was meant to feed millions of families. All patriots should call for the immediate rectification of our checks and balances on the government. The comprehensive list of executive orders need to be relinquished once we are no longer in a state of an emergency; the President has been strained to devise these over-reaching edicts due to the lack of effectiveness of the Legislative Branch. Also, our people have been in captivity with wars that Congress has never bothered to declare, using the loop-hole of a military police action which has plainly demonstrated that our separation of powers has been subverted. Last but not least, the Supreme Court has been gradually increasing its power and has been altered into legislating from the bench. Also, the ever-increasing power of centralized authority has been encroaching upon States' rights. How will this nation survive after its conversion to an oppressive system of Socialism? For a scholarly exposition on this controversy the audience is encouraged to read Volume Eleven of "A Chap's Book" by Brian Huff. These two works combined are intended to change the opinion of the reader to be in favor of our Constitutional Republic. Also, in the aftermath of the World Wars, the American people were charged with the rehabilitation of Europe and subsequently have been involved in Foreign Aid internationally of which power has not been granted by the Constitution to do so. This has been another major redistribution of wealth only globally, where the American taxpayer is forced into debt to alleviate the poverty of developing nations. We could call this cleverness on the part of the Communist who would take advantage of our pity and fiscal ignorance. Torture, or cruel and unusual punishment, did not end in the Enlightenment, but was carried on by popular fervor in various countries, especially Communist ones, mind you. The Left has constantly sympathized with Communist ideology, videlicet, unknowingly sometimes. The tales of tyranny have not gained the notoriety that they deserve in our classrooms in relation to our government because people seem to think we are an exception to the rule. The subjects of these Bills being passed appear to be for the mercy of those less fortunate, but the Devil is in the details. Conservatives' best method to blocking legislation ought to be to point out our enormous National Debt and their position to do so is now ripe for the taking. Our National Debt is embarrassing and as long as it continues any sane person should be supporting less expenditures. Remember atheism has poisonously reared its ugly head to our students for over half of a century, so do not expect morality to increase unless there is a religious revival which has happened before. This defiance to God will not help our people in finding solutions to their debts.

Truthfully, our elected officials can be said to be composed of a Communist majority, if one considers how their centralized system reflects upon their political philosophy. This book contains ample warnings about the dire consequences of the Left's agenda. The most important thing one could do is to acknowledge our Creator and pray instead of attempting to mystically transcend in a phony religion of secular humanism. The Left wants an absurd reconciliation between ecology and social equity where there will be a forced exodus from rural property into surveillance cities with even higher population densities. This is under the guise of environmentalism, where the cities will be surrounded by wild-lands for animals as people are forced into an impoverished equality to do the bidding of the "sustainable development" agenda. If there is any reluctance on the part of the rural citizen to participate, there will be energy restrictions and the infrastructure of the areas will be obliterated for wild-life. The New Age mysticism will be another facet of the globalist conquest, where Mother Earth will be intertwined with a goddess of heaven type figure, Mary. Any resignation one possesses will be observed by thine neighbors and reported in the cities filled with global citizens from mass immigration. People will be confronted by their own relatives regarding this allegiance

to the notions of tolerance and social justice.
If some of them indicate that you are not of
a sound mind (and this will come to mean,
politically) you will be taken away and your
property will be used to pay for your care
against your will. This system has been in
place for centuries, but was elevated after
the advent of the "Communist Manifesto"
happened with chemicals that shut-down
one's mental faculties, thereby silencing all
resistance. This will all be done officially
and your guns will be confiscated due to
behavior and beliefs. Negative actions that
are sexually immoral will be condoned and
become known as leisure. For sure, the
enslavers of mankind want the populace
debased and if someone seeks to change
this, they will be portrayed as the enemy of
tolerance. For certain, a chaste society is not
one of cowardice, but a villainous one is
over-run by fools. The cities filled with
foreigners will obstreperously massacre
Christians who will barely have their wits
about them after being betrayed to
psychiatric medication, some of which are
manufactured to lull the patient into
submitting to rape to avoid violent
retribution in prisons today! The transition
from a free society to a totalitarian one will

be unencumbered. We will have come a long way from biblical Common Law and the Magna Carta to the dictatorship formulated by those who would betray us for personal gain. If we are to be successful in recapturing the country's direction, the Executive, Legislative, and Judicial branches must all have their power reigned in. There can be no incentive to abide by the Constitutional limits unless there are criminal consequences that are effective in punishing our leaders. Unfortunately, legislators' right to not be arrested while in transit to and from Congress has been extended to their entire tenure of office which automatically shields the corrupt perpe-traitors. This should not be unsettling, if a politician blatantly violates the supreme law of the land, he should be arrested for his voting record. The equivalent to this should occur for the Supreme Court Justices which is impeachment and removal from their position. These perpe-traitors will no longer be as active if they face imprisonment and locking up Hillary is a good start to draining the swamp because she was a Senator who acted against the Constitution and was Secretary of State. Apparently, lawyers, etc. believe it takes a Constitutional scholar to interpret our document even though any literate fellow was meant to be capable of understanding it.

Chapter VI

Obamacare was the harbinger for universal health-care. Any kind of government arrangement like this is definitely Socialism. We should have considered reprimanding Barak Obama with impeachment for his Ponzi scheme, but now they are saying even he is too Conservative for the Democratic Party. It is no conspiracy theory that Trump's campaign had Deep State spies from within that Obama's Administration used which did everything falling short of intimidation. We should not forget the struggles the colonists dealt with in establishing a free and independent government. The rebel soldiers fought to break away from foreign rule and now we have a situation where we must submit to foreign powers in the United Nations without elected representation, where we are no longer independent. Virtually all we get is an ambassador like every other nation besides being able to veto legislation from

the assembly as a member of the Security
Council which includes Communist China.
This madness has all been instituted due to
the fears of war and yet they have went on
continuously since the inception of the
United Nations. Everywhere there is an
apprehension of the future with some
theories however implausible, affecting the
legislation of globalists. The constituency of
this country believes that the planet is
threatened by mankind and that the
population and industries must be curtailed
according to environmental extremists and it
plays right into the hands of the Communist
conspiracy. Global warming is totally
devoid of all logic and is just a scare tactic
used by scientists to receive funding for
more baseless research. Biology teachers are
cultivating our students with misinformation
about this and evolution is at the heart of all
of this nature-worship. The truth is that our
people have flourished in numbers at a
sustainable rate and it has pleased God that
we have been fruitful and multiplied. We
have been excellent stewards of his Creation
and have plenty of laws that protect nature
from being cruelly destroyed. We will not
receive retaliation from God for getting
married and procreating!

Maybe after exposing the results of Socialism and Communism in other countries, the younger generation can be converted to Capitalism. America is still at a clear advantage when it comes to profit because of her vast agricultural and mineral resources. There is plenty for our posterity if we keep it for ourselves. All proposals to share our wealth should be rejected, especially until we have paid off our National Debt. Our people need the relief and it would be erroneous to pander to the world's wants at this time. The burden these other countries place upon us is enormous and luckily Mr. Trump is ending some of this foreign aid. Our land has always been known as one of opportunity and prosperity due to God, its size, and our free-market economy. The pioneers were scattered all over the territory of the United States of America where they could farm unlike in crowded Europe where twice as many people live today in half the area. It was our destiny to manifest this beautiful country from sea to shining sea. An implementation of Federal regulations concerning land usage has made ranchers hostile to the government as evidenced by the armed stand-offs, recently. The domination the Federal government possesses is resented in the West, especially since it is hoarding property like in Nevada where over seventy-five percent of the land is owned by the government. Our farmlands have been a blessing to the people allowing them to be self-sufficient and industrious. American citizens no longer trust their own government and have become contentious with one another. We can tell these are the last days because the wife has turned on the husband and the children their parents, as predicted by the Bible where no one is loyal to the family. People are so confused, they are having operations to alter their physical appearances and sometimes their own gender. This is all a confirmation of the signs of the end times. Prophecy appears in both the Old and New Testaments and the Gospels even contain it, being spoken by Jesus Christ. The principles of the Bible are now being forsaken to our own detriment. Our land is now filled with degeneracy including drug use. It is no exaggeration to say that Satan is directly responsible and is guiding these perpe-traitors who are a threat from within. The author is coming to the conclusion based upon the direction of history that the Left always wins given enough time. It is like the entropy of civilization, however it is not a deliberate mandate from the people to partake in their own destruction. The current affairs addressed by the five corporations controlling the media express what the masses are soon to believe. There is this new term floating around called "white privilege" where any other explanation for discrepancies between equality that are not blamed on whites is considered racist. Is not it true that God has blessed us due to our faith in Him throughout the centuries when the rest of the world was pagan or Muslim? We have also received victory in armed conflict over the centuries and the Bible says "victory is of God". My guess is that the Left now alludes to "white privilege" because it seeks to push reparations for slavery and denies our birthright to possess the land our ancestors fought for. Scientists do not like to acknowledge that the theory of evolution contributed to all sorts of racism, especially in Nazi ideology. Some races were thought to be inferior because they were not as highly evolved. Of course, the Communist religion is atheism which is a world-view that believes it is justified by an adherence to the dogma of evolution. The

ravages of these Communist perpe-traitors
in their own countries was detestable. The
precursor to the rise of Communism was the
French Revolution and both consisted of a
vanquished upper class, where mass murder
took place all in the name of equality.

Attendance in these uprisings were
virtually compulsory, otherwise the
revolutionists turned on you with the
guillotine or firing squad once your loyalty
was suspected. These revolutionaries were
not gallant, but bloodthirsty, heretical mobs.
Somehow, they had no problem reconciling
terror with equality. No property was safe
from their plunder. Liberals are now
proposing that there are defects in our
Constitution as an excuse to circumvent its
supremacy, without even offering to amend
it. This consideration, passing an
amendment, is the only thing that makes it a
living document, so it should be interpreted
in a strict-constructionist fashion in order to
avoid the anarchy of the revolutions,
aforementioned. The preservation of society
was not at risk before the rebellion, as some
may claim, only after. The conduct of those
who gained power in these uprisings were
all despicable. Shame on anyone who wants

this to happen in our country, income inequality is real, but is no problem for the government to address, rather private philanthropy is the solution for economic disparities between the so called classes. The Left offers America nothing but despotism because that will be the natural result of their big government policies. It is always a possibility that we will be invaded by Communists like the Chinese now that they have successfully weakened us from within. It would take a lot of analysis as to how we should engage that sort of threat, for example do we use nuclear weapons, but we can be certain the Pentagon already has a plan? This is nothing to be frightened about because God will be on our side. Patriotism still runs deep and there would be open resistance by the common man even in sparsely populated areas, besides our military's protection. Our citizens' right to keep and bear arms offers us a double protection against an invasion. Our dependence on China is one of the reasons Trump was able to pass the steel tariffs in the name of defense because we are not prepared to fight a war with little manufacturing of war materials. Investments for these industries will grow if American business is able to compete with cheap over-seas products. Mr. Trump has had the "golden touch" on our economy. One of the reasons American products are so expensive compared to those manufactured over-seas is because of the dignity the American worker receives in wages and benefits. The laboring class is treated with more respect here than anywhere on the planet. In a way, they have been discontented with their wages in the past and have made the tariffs absolutely necessary due to their higher pay. At their onset, the ambition of the trade unions had been driven by the Communists. Part of the expectations of the Communist is to end all private property, especially in the means of production, but without the incentive of profit, industry crumbles. They believe that inheritances (that could be used for investment in businesses) demonstrate unfair advantages in our system of Capitalism. This hatred of the rich propels all the imagined desires of the perpe-traitors. They are ready to create all sorts of disturbances because of it including strikes, rioting, terrorism, and even insurrection. They are not loyal employees, but will betray their own livelihoods for their cause, believing that corporations are evil. They believe that Communist scum exhibit valor in standing up against all odds like an underdog. These extremists have lost all sensibility and are driven by jealousy and wrath. In order for them to prevail, they have admitted that violence is necessary and do not really believe in peaceful democracy to attain their goals. They were so clamorous against the Vietnam War because our adversaries were Communists who were for the working man, not because they actually desired peace like the hippies expressed. They are ruled by their own inadequate passions not by logic. Their own companies they work for are despised and actually their influence over the last century has enabled them to remain on a perpetual strike with some of them not working at all. Every time the people rise up under the banner of Communism, they are guilty of unconscionable depredations. No one should be oblivious to the hardships of the American worker, but charity is more of the solution not a centralized government bureaucracy. Watch for more coercive legislation that represses our freedom if the perpe-traitors of this philosophy take power because that is the only way they will be able to maintain it. They would readily initiate violent conflict because they believe the end justifies the means and that the moneyed influences are too powerful for them to merely put their trust in the electoral process like we do. The threat of these Leftists is serious and not just outlandish paranoia. We face impending doom if Socialists subvert the American system of free enterprise. Often, Socialist countries suffer from an amount of inflation that is shocking; for instance, imagine buying a loaf of bread with a fifty trillion dollar bill like in Zimbabwe. One should read the history of the malignant dictator Joseph Stalin of the USSR. Evidently, this is not even taught much in the public schools. That is not a good bargain for our tax-dollars, to have schools nurture children into becoming Democrats, but also to have them test miserably in comparison to the other civilized countries. It would be intelligent to get rid of the Department of Education and let the individual states handle education from here on out. We can still be encouraging when it comes to education in our country without the centralized authority of a Federal government. Also, private schools should get the recognition that they deserve for actually being successful in educating our nation's youth without the government. In private schools, the subject matter does not have to remain secular, prayer is an option, and students benefit from this. In private schools, one can learn what is moral, also, in a religious sense.

The Federal Government has abused its power by creating uniform educational standards in all fifty states. Our people need to be liberated from liberalism in our schools and media. The issue of nationalized transportation needs to be addressed, too, with Federally-funded infrastructure came a debate between the Whigs and Democrats as to whether or not it was Constitutional. This was one of the great controversies of the early nineteenth-century and it should have been decided that most Federally-funded infrastructure needs to be State funded. Each State should live up to its obligations when it comes to infrastructure because according to our Bill of Rights, it is their duty to build roads, etc. not the Federal Government. Arrangements should be made to dismantle the departments of Energy and Commerce, as well, under the same reasoning. We are supposed to have a limited de-centralized government, where the states are in

cooperation with one another in a set
number of things including the national
defense and the post office. If one State
upon scrutiny is deemed deficient or even
tyrannical, its citizens may leave, but what is
to become of us if all of the States fail
because we have put all the eggs in one
basket? In supporting this Constitutional
form of government the opposition might
say that States' rights does not work and that
is why the Articles of Confederation were
ended. This argument demonstrates a lack of
knowledge and neglects to address the
compulsive behavior that the centralized
authority has used against its own people.
The government is so vain it acts as though
our crops will not be cultivated without a
Department of Agriculture, too, but end
these massive bureaucracies and the budget
will be balanced. Perpe-traitors have
frustrated how the government was intended
to operate by adding all of this unnecessary
excess. These politicians should be confined
to the enumerated powers of our
Constitution and no, we do not need to listen
to them list all of the duties that these
departments have and how many people will
suffer without them. Their accumulation of
power has gone on long enough, their power

mirrors the Communists already and they are out for more. The government has squandered our resources and the rest of it does not have to be listed, like the Department of Labor, etc., that Libertarians would do away with. In fact, the income tax could be abolished with their plan as part of the possibilities and the people would accept this trade-off if given the opportunity.

Also, we need to end all foreign entanglements like George Washington recommended in his Farewell Address. It is not in our interest to compromise with everyone in the world, especially the Communists. Nevertheless, fear-mongers will preach against isolationism, but no one is advocating the absence of foreign diplomacy. As it has already been displayed, the United Nations is intrusively usurping our sovereign authority. Socialism is now in vogue among our nation's youth thanks to demagogues such as Bernie Sanders. Evidently, they do not even know what they are talking about, claiming they are anarchist one minute and Communist the next. Either way, these perpe-traitors in Antifa are guilty of seditions and have chanted for the end of America and her borders. However assiduous they may be at studying at their liberal colleges, Antifa probably smokes more marijuana than the hippies did and struggles to even think properly. That is why Trump's attestation that there were bad people on both sides of the protests at Charlottesville made perfect sense to people, except the media who scathed him for his comments. He clearly did not accept the idealism of either side, but then he was accused of supporting Nazis because a few of them were present, which is ridiculous. President Trump managed to defeat the political machinery of Washington, D.C. and he has suffered for it time and again. The convergence of the Democrats and the PerpeTraitors occurred around the rise of the Labor movement in the early twentieth-century. The zeal of this movement transformed America and its leader and founder in England, MacDonald, was a self-avowed Socialist. Of course, all of this has been forgotten, but those who do not learn from history are destined to repeat it. Fortunately, the author has been highly educated on the subject and is also a little fastidious when learning about the past. Yes, he too is a critic of the government's actions, but in different ways from what would be expected by a college student. The author does not romanticize about the Left as being virtuous as instructed, but rather has discovered how they have actually been the problem and instigators, historically. Be forewarned, this simple approach to historical analysis may supply one with plenty of resentment and bitterness, but so does wisdom.

The treacherous PerpeTraitors spread their discord at the work-place, in the churches, and at every American institution. They are guilty of calumnies against our leaders, past and present. Some of them, like George Soros, stir groups into a frenzy by financing civil unrest. They have disdained the United States of America and burned her flag in disrespect. Surpassing everything they have proposed in history, they claim only the government can save mankind from utter destruction because of pollution and are prepared to spend more money, controlling affairs more directly than ever before. These threats have only become serious due to their vast support among those indoctrinated by radical environmentalists who know nothing of realism, so to speak. The United States is

already in a quagmire due to the principles
of the Democratic Party or should we say
the absence of principles? The confrontation
between big government Socialism and
limited government Conservatism was
inevitable, but the odds are against the latter.
Twenty percent of the employed work-force
has a government position of some sort and
there are millions who receive money from
it without working, so we are facing an
insurmountable, negative possibility of any
reform however necessary it has become.
One thing is for certain, competition clearly
benefits our health-care industry which is
the best and one of the last profitable ones
left in our country. When it no longer faces
the trial of the free-market due to its being
shanghaied by the government, it will be
doomed to failure. There will no longer be a
worthy economic incentive to develop cures
or to provide the best care. Adam Smith's
invisible hand theory applies to health-care,
even, and there will be no remission for the
tax-payer that will cover how much the price
of it will increase with all of the
bureaucracy. Already, over half of the funds
for welfare are diverted from the recipients
to cover expenditures by the bloated
bureaucracy and this will get worse for

health-care, a waste that is not justifiable. Your file under such a system and how obedient you are to a government doctor will become an impingement upon your freedom or privacy. We will suffer from an infestation of health protocols and everyone will be given a social credit score like in Communist China, if we give into Socialized medicine. Do you really want the government through doctors telling you not to smoke, drink, or eat things in an effort to save you with punishments like in other countries for disobedience to Big Brother. Instead of a free-citizen, you will not escape the life of a convict where the world becomes your prison. Give me liberty or give me death by cancer! Just imagine Commie psychiatric care where everyone gets to participate and you are considered a bigot against the mentally ill for not admitting to the government's diagnosis. Just ponder damnation as a grade received, given by a government monitor because in China people are prevented from using transportation due to low social credit scores.

Chapter VII

These authoritarian perpetraitors should stand to be condemned by all freedom loving Americans. They would have you believe, like the Prussians believed before launching an invasion in World War I, that the government is the moral authority, not God, when it comes to what is right and wrong. Of course, these actions went unfinished and the Nazi Socialists took the place of the militaristic Prussians in World War II. World War I did inflame the German autocracy into retaliation, especially after it was forced to pay reparations. Eventually, Hitler came to power, with no conscience, becoming a tyrant just like the kind our Constitution was designed to prevent. The assumption is that it can never happen here and yet the groundwork has already been lain. The Liberal sound-bites need to be clarified in a debate as to what would be their repercussions financially and for our liberty. Frequently, the media asking questions gives the Liberals a pass on these subjects, as though they should not be a concern. They play into the hands of the political PerpeTraitors allowing the people to accept their assurance as though there is no danger behind what they are proposing. The expansive government is assaulting our rights, but so far it has only penetrated small factions of the population, which is the kind of majority-rule tyranny that the Founders vouchsafed against.

The remedies to this situation would include Constitutional reform, not a reformation of the Constitution, but a reformation of the government, so that it is obedient to the document. Many perpetraitors will be dismayed once they discover that they are being fired, prosecuted, or impeached for betraying our country. No doubt, they will practice evasion with legal tactics and loose interpretations of our Constitution to preserve their radicalized entrenchment within the United States government. The plaintiff in these cases will be the people and there must be an unbiased jury. The sense of urgency must be great and this book I hope will be pivotal in gathering public sentiment against the Deep State's betrayal of the people. The people must become zealous in restoring their liberties while there is still an opportunity. The terrible government now has the potential through its size and strength to become the ultimate tool of oppression. Mankind needs Americans to resist all tyranny and the New World Order. We are tiring of the excuses as to why the government has been in debt for decades with no major war to justify it.

All of these unconstitutional acts originated in a loose interpretation of the Constitution that focuses on a single clause that states the government may do things that are "necessary and proper". There is a consensus among scholars educated at Liberal colleges that this is appropriate, but their opinions are all in retrospect of the policies adopted by the government that utilize this clause in their defense. In order for the enumerated powers to prevail against Federal expansion, the second part of the clause should be examined because it can already be argued that most of the bureaucracy is not absolutely "necessary". So what exactly is "proper" while maintaining the Constitutional restraints on the government? The definition of "proper" could mean right or decent and the Founders were leaving a provision within the text for some operations not listed, maybe. To interpret the clause, one has to acknowledge the context of the rest of the document. Why list the functions of the government deliberately if one word "proper" is meant to magically allow it to do everything? That would not make any sense and would be an injustice. Our country was founded upon the idea of a very limited government and all of its actions not "necessary and proper" outside of its listed powers are un-Constitutional and should be left up to the individual States to execute. Everyone knows that this is the logical conclusion for those who would have faith in the intentions of our Founders. The differences of opinion arise from what is considered pragmatic or popular that politicians are unwilling to abandon. The Constitutional standard must be met and nowhere does it mention universal health-care or free college tuition. The same people who disagree with absolute truths which are fundamental in the rights of man will argue for some sort of relativism when it comes to what should be legal for the government. Any real arguments based on Constitutional law that defend the expansion of our government in the twentieth-century paralleling those of the rest of the world are insufficient, at best.

One of the bases for justice is the written law that allows all to know of the laws put forth beforehand. The Constitution is not only useful, but essential for these ends, so that the people are aware of how the government is warranted to act. Take away this contract with the people, claiming that some new aspect of the government is plausible without an amendment, and there will be trouble. The elasticity of the Constitution has already been refuted, I characterize it as such because the "necessary and proper" terminology is known as the elastic clause. An example of something not outlined in the Constitution that would not be prohibited is the Air Force because it is within the context of the Framers who foresaw that things "necessary" for the defense might arise. Other things under the category of defense that were not envisioned, but apply to the elastic clause are the accomplished Department of Homeland Security and the Southern Border Wall in progress. It must be remembered that Mexico has plotted our destruction in the past with France in the nineteenth-century and Germany during World War I. We have overcome these threatened invasions, but did have a war with her prior to our Civil War, so it is not like she is entirely peaceful, but wants back the Southwest as evidenced by all of the millions of Mexicans who have thus far only "settled" the area.

All members of the military and elected officials (Federally) have chosen to take an oath to defend the Constitution of the United States and it is a shame that most have been persuaded to overlook its true meaning. They believe in something now that is a mere resemblance to this great document like how Christmas has become devoid of Christianity in a way or Easter. The genius of our system is based solely upon the Constitution and it is the PerpeTraitors' worst enemy because it stands in the way of their goals. The persecution of Russian clergy did arise during the Leftist Bolshevik Revolution and I have viewed a photograph of one of their machine guns on top of a building mowing down a civilian crowd that included women and children like the Vegas shooter who was found with Antifa literature. They have offered no substitute to the document which would at least be within the realm of lawfulness and have afforded us no amendments to coincide with their abuse of power. Right now, we are fighting these PerpeTraitors tooth and nail for the preservation of our Second Amendment. The difficulty is that they are not playing by the same rules and think they can just ignore it. The right to bear arms by the individual has already been ruled as being secure by the Supreme Court recently, so the old Liberal argument that it applies only to the militia is erroneous. To avoid addressing this issue too garrulously, one more thing will be stated and that is, the Liberals are totally against the militia movement anyways and would not defend their rights to exist according to the Second Amendment either, ironically.

Without taking these PerpeTraitors to task, another dastardly alternative to their apprehension will unfold. A supreme and indestructible oppression will become the bane of civilization around the world. The amount of graft and corruption that those involved with the Federal Government are guilty of is uncanny. This valuable country has been lost in blackmail and every other sort of grievous crime. The decay of morality is evident to all without an appreciable advantage being acquired to make up for it. The Left's contention with racists has formed into animosity of anyone even suspected of it during otherwise peaceful demonstrations that turn ferocious. These shouting matches that de-evolve into mob violence are quite the spectacle. People totally innocent walk away with blood drawn from rocks, bats, etc. These spontaneous eruptions of violence will be used to catalyze a tyrannical reaction upon our right to peaceably assemble. Just think, the governor of Virginia summoned a state of emergency when only one person died, which possibly was an accident. This was conducive to the PerpeTraitors authoritarian plans to appear to be as intolerant of intolerance as possible, making a mountain out of a mole hill.

It is none other than Lucifer who led the Bolsheviks to revolt and after Germany's defeat in World War I, they intended to conquer all of Europe. His primeval rebellion has been the inspiration for all sin in the world. Envying God Himself, Satan teaches mankind to resent just authority. These Red rascals sent Russian women to the trenches and then cowardly signed a peace deal with Germany in the middle of the First World War. After they had a formidable showing against the Nazis, the British drew up plans for invading the Communists in the aftermath of World War II. Then they were permitted to build up a Doomsday nuclear arsenal of which the technology was lifted by Communist agents from America according to some sources, although the Leftist establishment teaches that they developed atomic capability independently by coincidence. These are not defamatory remarks against American prudence, there was actually Soviet agents within the United States government during the Roosevelt Administration and the idea is not that far-fetched considering that they were our allies against Nazi Germany. The cordiality between Roosevelt and the Communists is represented by all of his new government programs that were deemed un-Constitutional by the Supreme Court until he tried to add more justices that backed his policies, like a dictator. His superiority as a demagogue was demonstrated by his numerous terms in office and because of him the President is now limited to two terms, which was a precedent that began with George Washington.

The emergence of these PerpeTraitors cannot be confined to any one era in modern history. An embittered middle class of trade guilds developed in the towns of Medieval Europe and that was possibly a precursor to what has occurred overtime. For centuries, the noblemen and royalty reigned over peasants and ideas of liberty were expressed by noblemen in relation to the ruling sovereign. Any enthusiasm for a theory of the evolutionary progression of rights may be disproven in England if one looks at how the Anglo-Saxons lived in comparison to the risen feudalistic Normans. Supposedly, the Saxons would divide local control over government type affairs to representatives in groups known as the Witan. Even if one goes back to the birth of Christ, Britons were hardly in a state of savagery like the Romans had claimed due to the fact that they were enemies on the battle field. This was a revision of history on the part of the conquering Romans whose own empire declined because of their growing effeminacy and immorality. The rise of knowledge in modern history should not be seen as a rise in intelligence because we have exceptional literary works from one thousand years before Christ like Homer's

Odyssey and the Old Testament, so do not
fall into the delusion that Leftist opinions
are more evolved because they have
developed more recently. It should not be
beyond one's comprehension that our
Republic with a Senate was conceived after
similar democratic republics that existed
before the time of Christ. Until the Israelites
thought it satisfactory that they should have
a monarchy, they were ruled by judges and
representatives of tens, hundreds, etc. to
interpret the laws of Moses.

These PerpeTraitors have distorted the
truth about Capitalism for so long. It is their
conviction that property should be forcibly
shared through the government and whether
it be half of your income or property or all
determines whether you're a Socialist or
Communist. Any leader of these movements
is an impostor. Leadership over Liberals
requires much vanity because the elected
Liberals have already heard the truth and
seen the consequences, first hand, so they
are without excuse when compared to some
of their supporters. Our Constitution need
not suffer any further degradation. No doubt,
the perpetraitors have been conspiring
against us, determining when it just might be

the opportune time to become more aggressive against our liberties. They have probably calculated in a scientific way just how many more tragedies the American people will take before they side with public safety over freedom. It is not enough that they capture the man guilty of the crime and put him to death, they have to make everyone believe that they should suffer, too, because one man has abused his privilege. We need an armed populace in public as well as in private homes who can vigorously put up a defense against a mass-shooter. The Democrats are now pushing a stubborn agenda that is false, that has caused Al Gore to lose his own state while running for President, and displays that they want absolute control over society.

Besides the "Communist Manifesto", Karl Marx is responsible for writing "Das Kapital" which bemoaned the labor situation claiming that the laborer deserved more. Basically, the Capitalist earned a set amount off of each worker, so that worker should be given more, when in reality the strategical choice would be for the Capitalist to keep the price of his product as low as possible for it to sell against his competitors. You cannot really go anywhere with his commercial theory because it would just raise prices, if all wages were driven up across the board. Determining how things are priced is a natural element of trade which can be affected by tariffs. A phenomena of higher wages would have to be forced either by strikes or the government and eventually the whole world would have to be Communist just for one Communist country to succeed. That is why it is no mystery that the PerpeTraitor needs world conquest to complete his goals. Meanwhile, we could have just kept things the ordinary way; the Communist way would result in very little change over-all for the wealth of the laborer. Leftists have become aggressive and are not the proponents of merely civil disobedience. They should be condemned at every turn with all of the forms they represent. Their religion has become sacrilege.

To presume that a multimillionaire is guilty because he is rich of oppressing the worker and profiting off of the backs of the poor is all Leftist rhetoric. In his defense, he used his advantages to supply the needs of the laborers he employed, who if they had their way might have prevented him from employing anyone, at all. Defiance to one's employer should be punished according to how much profit they have caused him to lose. The repression of strikes, mob-violence, and rioting should be done with force. The Savior preached against workers who were discontented with their wages. The only way the Liberals will win is if Conservatives remain complacent with the status quo which is admittedly their strength because maintaining the present circumstances is how they oppose change the best. What if the change has already taken place like in Congress and Parliament? Conservatives do not really have to adapt, but rather should practice their faith with more devotion and then an emanation of good-will must result with loyalties to the ancient establishments of private property, etc. that must increase in law enforcement and the military. The trial of life that every Christian must endure will be extended to encompass social interaction and politics, not just between the temptations of devils and the believer. We should place no limitations on the power of God because with Him all things are possible. This prior statement is not meant to detract from spiritual warfare against the Devil, for even only one sin brings upon much evil.

Think of the situation as a voyage where eventually the PerpeTraitors will mutiny to split the ship's booty, if at that point the righteous man will not resist, flog, and execute the pirates, the threats will become more frequent across the sea. Any such venture will fail if there is no one to stand for the Ten Commandments; thou shalt not steal, envy, kill which are all things radical Leftists are for when placed into fervent action. When someone deserves rebuke and righteous indignation one must not spare him, but must hold a commanding tone. The Liberals also complain about the effects of processed meats, genetic engineering, hormones, and antibiotics in our food, so when they asked me to sign a petition against a major meat company in Chicago, I went right to their headquarters. They wanted people to be terrified of these products and I pleaded with them to leave the meat industry alone, stating I was an author. They, who preyed upon the general public's fears, asked me if I had any writing that pertained to the issue and I just so happened to have had a copy of an essay I wrote on "The Jungle". "The Jungle" sparked interest in regulating the meat-packing industry when it debuted, but in my essay I focused on how the work was Socialist propaganda which is plain to see. The author was a member of the Socialist Party and consciously included political rhetoric from that party into the plot. They made a copy of my essay and began murmuring once I told them not to mess with the meat company, stating that their mass produced products were necessary for people across our country and served them well at an inexpensive price. They bid me to part ways like what I said caused them affliction because to the Left, the corporation is the enemy. They think that it is taking advantage of the consumer with an inferior product that could be hazardous and no doubt some of them were vegetarians or in conformity with Kosher beliefs. They looked like they were mainly college kids, not Orthodox Jews though, who needed to be taught what is needed to feed a country and what a service this company does to provide for the protein needs in the military-industrial complex lifestyle that many are ignorant of. Protesting a brand name meat company would be considered unconventional, but I hope one can see how it equates to the other tactics of the Left. The Communists will make any excuse to go after business and to weaken the military-industrial readiness of our people. It is amazing how they are even trusted with any occupation and yet they have found a way to infiltrate every segment of our society, thus converting their radicalism into mainstream thought.

One should clearly be critical of the veracity of the statements made by Leftists and often the whole truth is not told by the media. With taxation, one could technically say consent has not been given by the payer because a large voting bloc of the Democrats pays no taxes because of poverty and the ones who pay the most, are often for those Republicans who are for large tax-cuts. Those who offer exultation for the Democrats are against the rich, but the rich are not against the poor as much as the poor are against them and provide charity. The poor are inclined to be like this because of Leftist propaganda, but this resentment is unjustified unless the rich person is actually oppressive. Make no mistake, Conservatives are not for respecting a rich person more

than a poor one usually and the author
believes wage earners should not have to
wait two weeks for a pay check, but should
receive them more frequently if poor. The
book's viewpoint just expresses that the rich
are unfairly treated by Leftists probably due
to the majority-rule ideology that the
Founders feared. The Congress is meant to
filter popular opinion, not to mirror it,
otherwise we would hold referendums on
everything. Today it is common to hear
pretensions about our country being a
democracy, but this is neither correct nor
was it intended to be so as evidenced by the
Electoral College, even, that was meant to
safeguard against ill-begotten democratic
sentiments. The disputations in Congress
need to be resolved according to what is
right, not according to what will get their
members re-elected. The opinions of the
majority may be just as much of an enemy
to liberty as two-thirds of the populace were
who did not rebel against Great Britain and
assert their rights. The British may have had
the same kind of arrogance that our current
leaders do, with over-taxation and gun
confiscation. The minute-men were
protecting their right to bear arms at

Lexington and Concord where the Red-coats were ordered to seize weapons.

Chapter VIII

The Perpetraitors are guilty of encroachment upon our rights. With each extension of the Federal Government that does not pertain to the original powers circumscribed by the Framers of the Constitution, the Tenth Amendment in our Bill of Rights is trampled on. Besides the old monarchies who still preserved some resemblance of liberty, the Bolsheviks were the ones guilty of causing totalitarian abuses and were characterized as being mentally disturbed by our leaders. To say that any new violation of our rights here are unprecedented is to totally ignore the abuses that have occurred by Socialists like Nazis and Communists. Yes, by identifying them as Socialists, this would be correct because Hitler, Lenin, Trotsky, Stalin, and Mao were all purportedly for the organization of the working class against the wealthy establishment, to say the least. The only exceptions to their similarities, or actually the major difference is that Hitler railed against the Jews for controlling the establishment and the Soviets were led by some Jews to revolt, Trotsky being the prime example. Hitler's racism defined his regime, no doubt, but because the Leftists had power across Europe and America, he has been called a Fascist. Whatever the perceptions of Fascism, Communism, and Socialism are on the Right and Left, the dictionary holds a very similar definition of all three, only one of the features of Communism is that everyone shares the products of the government owned businesses. Now that that has been straightened out, it should be stated that both Communism and Fascism are types of Socialism which means the government ownership of the means of production and distribution. The Russians were not known as Fascists, but rather took Socialism even farther; Fascism has nothing to do with race, rather it is distinguished by innumerable regulations on businesses; Antifa claims Trump and his supporters are Fascists, when in reality, Trump has ended more regulations than any other President by Executive Order. The futility with arguing the facts with Antifa masked thugs should be apparent to anyone who sees this terrorist organization in action.

Now that President Trump has been investigated since the time he took office, the PerpeTraitors think they finally have him on two impeachable offenses. He is calling them crazy, saying he did nothing wrong while being charged with "abuse of power" and "obstruction of Congress". This is like some edict from Leningrad and the Leftists were not allowing him to face his accuser or have his lawyer present during the inquiry. First, it was the Russian hoax where he supposedly conspired with Russia to get elected, now this totally political chicanery where even a murderer gets more rights than the President of the United States. Why bother to say he did either of those things, when they are not even illegal? For the sake of briefness, the first charge is too vague for there to be a law against, the second one is too political, and I have already written about what he did in regards to his attempt to get officials to investigate international corruption by a leader of the Democratic Party. The real perpetrators are Joe Biden, treasonous Nadler, Schiff, and Pelosi, that is the case. Although the country would benefit from them being prosecuted for acting under the broad definition of the term treason, the Constitution still protects them in that they are Congressmen (which would require a very loose interpretation of a Constitutional clause) and that treason may only apply to those who have aided or become an enemy in arms against the United States. Though, it has been addressed previously in a like manner, it does not hurt to clarify the facts again. Once he was accused of all of this about a telephone call from a person with second or third-hand information, his release of the literal conversation's transcript should have been adequate. Of course, the Democrats and the media were already wanting him impeached before the phone call, but none of the facts matter to those who now possess dominion over the House of Representatives. Do they really believe they should do something just because they can, that is sophomoric?

The Democratic debates could be characterized as a sideshow with some of their leading candidates admitting publicly that they are Socialists. Anyone who made the connection between the Democrats and Socialists was considered a Right-wing extremist only twenty years ago, but guess who was right? Respectfully, Mr. Biden did say something patriotic at the end of one, but he was the first one to do so. Let us analyze his patriotism, though, within the framework of what he actually said. Basically, he maintained something like, this is America and we can do anything. However glorious that may have sounded, no we cannot literally do anything. Also, it reflected upon his political philosophy that the government should get to do anything that is possible. What a fabulous notion, it is just something trendy to be said like "have pride in yourself", only pride is a sin. The other point that patriotism was seldom expressed should be noted before it is written here that at least Biden attempted to credit this country with a type of virtue.

These saboteurs are trying to wreck our people's very existence however they can manage it. Their initiative is one of scandalous bribery, embezzlement, etc. and when they are caught publicly, it is just the tip of the iceberg. The elite are innocent in that they may have been initially set-up by Communist pigs, but are forever beholden to them to save their own skins. A quest for illegal actions for every police man has begun and the more of them there are, the more crime will be discovered or fabricated to collect fines to feed them. Back in history, there was no police force, just a sheriff, but supplanting them now would mean chaos for law-abiding citizens. Why, because there has been unprecedented crime that has increased exponentially? Our people are in dire need of discipline as evidenced by the prison population. Sure, no one is taken to the gallows anymore, but why spend so much money on executions that are necessary when the Bible says that the man who hangs from a tree is cursed, him and his offspring for seven generations? Meanwhile, what are the perpetraitors saying to sabotage our law and order: end capital punishment, lower sentencing, free the prisoners, etc.? Although not visible, guess whose idea that is, in the ear of the Leftist... the criminal. They venture to assume that the prisoner is a victim of the system of Capitalism we hold dear to however imperfect. Try an expression of freedom, but does one ever see old ladies exhibit distaste for the government en masse or are we not ruled by this segment of the population who is a major voting bloc? Wear a blindfold in regards to their faults and never correct them, but know that they are the back-bone of the way things are. The "progress" that opposes this portion of the political landscape will nearly always be worse. In particular, they can be blamed for what has transpired thus far. They are dignified compared to the fairer sex of today's youth, but no one is free from guilt when it comes to sin, specifically, and complacency, overall, when it comes to the dissolution of a limited government. Though, the ship of state is burning, do not jump overboard, rather douse the flames while we still have a relative blessing from God, perhaps.

The author is not accusing old ladies of any crimes, but they are likely on Social Security, Medicare, and food stamps, so why are the youthful countrymen not challenging this, but rather asking for more for people like them, when it comes out of the wage earners' pockets? One has to remember that times have changed and that a large segment of the population, age 18-35, is still living with their parents. The older generation stood by as their rights were conceded to the Federal Government a hundred times, but the solution is to keep the angry young man fenced in with pills, unemployment, and dependency on the government that everyone would rather not have. Would you rather have lived with your own money or that given to you by a bureaucracy is a simple question with an obvious answer? It was also a moot point for even your grandfather, most likely, who was able to support his entire nuclear family. People would like to ask what went wrong, but are hushed if they agree with the premise of this book. Due to our imperfection, which is an understatement, Christ will be coming down on us literally; whether we are to be his target along with the others is yet to be seen. However harrowing this may be to some sinners, Jesus Christ is ruling above our leaders and even Queen Elizabeth II acknowledges this fact. Despite all we know about tolerance, Pharisees literally had Him abducted after He was in tears and prayer to His Almighty Father and had our soon to be resurrected King crucified.

Jesus' crucifixion for standing up for what is right shows what the establishment will do to a man. Do not place it beneath these PerpeTraitors to manufacture a crisis such as a recession in order to weaken us further.

They may use disruption to confiscate our weapons like how a Democrat of Virginia proposed calling out the National Guard against counties who do not comply with gun control who have voted themselves Second Amendment sanctuaries. Sheriff Jenkins of Culpepper County said he intends to deputize thousands from the general population to ensure our right to bear arms. The State government recently became dominated by the Democrats due to the cities, but most of the counties, like every State are Republican that vote against gun control measures more often. The perpetraitors would like to see the termination of private gun ownership as it has happened in other countries. As a solution to the troubling small arms treaty created by the United Nations to oppress the world with global gun control, President Trump withdrew from it. The actions of the United Nations would agitate more Conservatives if they were actually well-known and the perpetraitors are stronger there than in our country. Look for the U.N.'s influences to grow because of this and for the Democrats to call upon it more and more to resolve local issues in America against our will. The United Nations will demand our subjection if our own government does not first. The lust for international control over us has finally been defeated in England with the Conservatives having their greatest success in thirty years after supporting the referendum to leave the European Union. It should not be that astonishing since the Perpetraitors within the E.U. have been for unbridled immigration and foreign control over sovereign nations without democratic representation. The only rightfully instituted world government will be the Kingdom of God ruled by Jesus Christ. This will be the final triumph over these PerpeTraitors. Both the European Union and the United Nations presume that their decisions overrule the Common Law statutes of the United Kingdom and the United States of America. Indubitably, our cousins, the British, will fight alongside us in Armageddon.

The origins of our laws are based on the Pentateuch and we are aligned diplomatically with those who possess Israel where this battle has been prophesied to take place. We have been predestined as God's people, but the author of this does not adhere to all of the things said about

Doomsday. Rather, he interprets the prophecies of the Bible from a Historicist view like the first Protestants. Christ will courageously lead us to victory over the nations of the world in the aforementioned final battle to avenge His martyred saints. The faithless Perpe-Traitors will have the world celebrating in the streets over the deaths of two witnesses that dared to preach to sinners. With the Historicist interpretation of Scriptures, mankind has been fulfilling the prophecies of the Bible throughout history that so many use an example for us to withdraw and hide and the end times actually began after Christ's resurrection.

But enough with theology, it suffices to say that the pre-millennial mantra of the rapture was put into place by other perpetraitors for the purpose of persuading Christians that they should retire from the fight to save themselves. The Lord warned that he who seeks to save his life shall lose it. There is a spiritual side to many things and these perpetraitors may feel that they are doing the right thing, but the road to hell is paved with good intentions. They no longer possess loyalty to our country, but rather to the world government which many

Christians think will come into being at the Apocalypse with the Beast as its ruler. This may seem far-fetched to those who consider themselves reasonable, of course. You do not have to be religious to imagine a one world government, especially if terrorism dramatically increases and people feel helpless.

One way to fight a coming one world government is to make sure that our country's sovereignty remains intact. Any international agreement that forces us to obey something within our own borders that we should be deciding ourselves is an attack on our independence. To subvert justice here, the Deep State criminals will move into international crime, so that they can claim they are above the jurisdiction of the U.S. that is putting pressure on them. Public servants are not above the law, but in fact should face higher scrutiny regarding it. Also, it is a form of treason to abdicate the powers of our government to another authority. We are already overwhelmed with draconian laws from our own government, why submit to those international decrees without elected representation? And yes, the United Nations vexes us with "taxation without representation" indirectly because we are forced to fund it with revenue from our taxes. As you can see, Conservatives do not need to buttress their arguments with endless statistics and facts to get their points across, just bringing to light a few things on each subject is startling enough to be effective in convincing the reader. We do not need quotations from perpe-traitors or from reference material to show what is right. Although, it may be realized that most of the author's publications that are non-fiction are scholarly with ample citations. Be delighted that this text is not burdened by other sources to bolster mere claims, but the persuasive opinions are able to stand alone. That is how this book is unique from the other works of "A Chap's Book" series, a man's conscience will aid the author in gaining significant approval for these view-points.

As it currently stands, the laws and regulations of America are like a labyrinth. Ironically, faith in Constitutional law has faltered coinciding with a thousand laws that no one is even aware of that essentially water down right from wrong. The iniquity of the U.S. tax code, which encompasses

more than a four feet high stack of
voluminous books, basically provides a
system where anyone might be guilty, but no
one knows and it basically defeats the
purpose of written law. It is common for
perpetraitors to assume that if one has
money worthy to be taxed, it must have been
attained illegally in some fashion and that
the property owner must be made to confess.
Be prepared to face a succession of
questions from people who want a piece of
the pie, like crooked investigators, and the
best policy is to say nothing ever because
you will be surrounded by perpetraitors or
those who can easily be made to betray you.
Once you begin to talk after amazingly
experiencing anything profitable fancy
yourself on the run. If you are successful in
running far enough and keep talking amidst
wire-taps and interviews, it is inevitable you
will have to offer a sacrifice of somebody
else who has talked to the authorities.
Sooner or later, if you can talk your way into
running for the shelter of public office,
maybe you can disclose how the
Communists have made Capitalistic gain
nearly illegal in our country. You will be
watched by those who want to bribe or just a
paying contract that is not to one's

advantage due to favors, etc. Some people have thanked God that they have labored with their hands for their livelihood and stayed clear of the organized crime, corruption, and addictions that fuel the perpetraitors. The Communist conspiracy is deeper and darker than one could ever imagine and really the best thing to do about it is to pray.

Evil is predominant and you will find few who have not strayed from the straight and narrow. The typical perpetraitor does not have any direct knowledge about what goes on behind the scenes. The nobility's interactions with them in England must occur from time to time, but with all of their money left, they are rather helpless in comparison to the power they once held. Anything lucrative for them might arise through connections, not owning vast estates. They still have enough where they do not have to settle for things cheap and the perpetraitors think the noblemen are the perpetrators for not sharing everything and becoming commoners. It is only natural for them to regard the commoner as dubious because no one knows their intentions and they may be a danger to their person or fortune. It would not be preposterous to foresee a possible plot against them due to the perpetraitors against free government, perhaps paranoia could be more justified with wealth or power.

All of this propaganda against corporations has led to merciless verdicts against them in the court of law. The psychology of the jury, being biased now against the wealthy and business results in enormous amounts of restitution for supposed victims. People think they are characterized by greed, so when a lawns-keeper ended up with cancer after using a product, he was awarded tens of millions of dollars. Industries now have warning labels on dangerous products, as this one did, and there was not even a way to be certain that the cancer was caused by the lawn-care chemical. These tort cases are one of the last ways to make real money in this country, mainly because the jurors are not judicious enough to protect companies from frivolous law-suits. This is just another example of the civilized forms of theft.

The reason why it is a conspiracy amongst the perpetraitors is because everything has to be secret due to their criminal elements and the rejection they would face if outwardly expressing Communism. For the time being, the majority of Americans are still philosophically against them, although Communist's counterpart, Socialism, is gaining in popularity. Another one of their masks is "Liberation Theology" which came into play after the face of Communism was tarnished. Their supporters liken their own leadership to Robin Hood, though they are not noble, brave, or handy with a weapon. I guess people no longer know how cruel a dictatorship may be and they imagine that whatever type of Communism they adopt will somehow be different like a utopia. Why suffer the compulsions of a dictator and please realize that the more the centralized government expands, the more power one would have? Americans have a responsibility to keep the power in the hands of the States or the people, so that it better reflects their will, thereby satisfying them politically. Opinions differ depending on the region and people are discouraged now that things have become more uniform across the United States. One locality may have the opposite views of another, but if the locals have control over the feeding of indigents, etc. it gives more people power rather than a few from Washington, D.C. That type of government, ruled by a few over hundreds of millions, tends to impose on peoples' lives. The fact is, Washington, D.C. has become over-reaching and has made folks dependent upon her in order to supplement her own power.

Chapter IX

After reading this book and understanding the basics of Leftist ideology, one may no longer have to view politics as a perplexity. The work is not vague, although it avoids cumbersome details, and it allows the political spectator to realize why each Democrat holds the position on each issue that they do by getting to the foundation of the matter. It is to be expected that Liberals will disagree with most if not all of this analysis and it is not meant to cater to them. To point out that we are being subjected to propaganda is admittedly extreme as is describing our government as having the symptoms of a Communist nation. The material dealt with in this work is not very encouraging, but most Conservatives already understand what has taken place, especially because the media does not give their interpretation to any issue these days, being completely one-sided. Upon examination, it is totally logical to be critical of the media, like the President and his supporters are, because it is a Liberal bastion like our educational system. The perpetraitors are being very careful in their word-choice while controlling information and themes in entertainment to benefit their own causes, fearing the people if they are not controlled by Liberal opinions. It is like they are impressing the general population with Leftist rhetoric without them even noticing. It is hard to say who will have the ability to see through it and think independently. I hope one will find clarity in the way the truth has been presented thus far. The author is not beholden to corporations or the Liberal establishment and has only taken one oath in order to join a fraternity, so his motives for writing this are purely for the good as he sees it. Of course, the author wonders who in the community may be open to "PerpeTraitors" while coming to the realization that it will do no good if only like-minded individuals are exposed to it. It should be concluded that the book will move Conservatives farther to the Right than they may be used to because it adheres to Libertarian ideas when it comes to fiscal Conservatism.

A lot of times, Libertarians and Conservatives have shared beliefs on fiscal policy, but only some Republicans like a century ago would have been in congruence with those Libertarians' views today. Not to get side-tracked, the vote for the advent of the Social Security Administration was passed by a bipartisan vote, whereas Libertarians are still against it to this day like some Republicans were for Constitutional reasons. The program cannot be declared Socialism Security because each worker pays into it during his lifetime when compared to other proposals where the rich would pay the brunt of the cost of a program. It has relieved many people of the responsibility of having to save for their own retirement. Despite the benefits of this program, it is still un-Constitutional and before its arrival, the elderly had to depend on their children, mostly, and also were able to have them listen to what they were told. It is apparent now that there have been major changes in society because the elderly are isolated from their families living independent lives. Families are no longer dedicated to tradition, customs, and religion under the guidance of the older generation. This may sound controversial, but could this be what the Communists foresaw happening with Social Security to their advantage, having positions in the U.S. government during FDR's Administration?

The author, here, is not accusing Democrats of wanting to practice Stalinist techniques on the American people, the speculations are pointing to the fact that the type of government they have pushed for will be capable in the future of murderous tendencies. All it takes is for one tyrant to hold office, for the centralized government has already been empowered dramatically for the last century. Perhaps now, the lifespan of our free Republic has been shortened due to all of the debt that has increased to fund Socialism. Although the people are not hankering for war, we have been maintaining a military capacity to invade other countries and if there was some way to avoid nuclear war, would we start an empire for financial gain? The oil fields in the Middle East are invaluable, we already have a military presence there, and some of their nations could be easily defeated. In all honesty, even though we would benefit, this is not going to happen under the system of world governance of the United Nations because we would have to have some sort of permission or be considered a belligerent. I would be surprised if any of the readers would have even considered an invasion which is well within our capability because it is not part of their mental conditioning.

America is fortunate in that it is still the freest country on Earth. When pointing out its flaws, I am not complaining and would rather love it than leave it. For most of us, we inherited this country from our ancestors who toiled hard to make it what it is today. Once we settled the land all the way to the Pacific Ocean, it was a fulfillment of our people's destiny. The first settlers of the nation were not wicked, but God-fearing, devout Christians. Thus, they were allowed to flourish with the blessings of God. What America needs is a reclamation from sin, so that our right to multiply upon the land is restored. The media has entirely wrecked us with nudity, lies, etc. that make us give in to moral relativism and provide us with excuses to commit fornication and adultery because it is okay on television. This observation is accurate; Satan has instigated sin to have the best country in the world weakened to where God will no longer defend her. The Devil has been instrumental in spreading the bloodshed of Communism across the globe and he and the perpetraitors will not be satiated until it engulfs America. Notice not only the decline in morals, but also the rise in the occult. Hollywood uses it to create a national fear of evil when in reality, Christians should be fearing God. The separation of church and state has now somehow been used to defend Satanism. A court decided that the military must allow witchcraft to be practiced on base along with many other heinous decisions. This displays that our legal system is broken. As a consequence of all of those changes, God may turn his back on us. Even the simplest notion of equality has now been misconstrued into affirmative action, hate crime legislation, and maybe reparations for slavery. Anyone preaching that these are examples of equality is teaching about myths of extra privilege for minorities. Justice should be blind when it comes to race, as far as whether or not a person is guilty of a crime that can be committed by any race. These are instances of superficial laws that cannot solve the problem of hatred. They were meant to cater to minorities, who vote in a larger proportion for Marxist candidates. The activity of Leftists across the globe reflect Marxism and that is why the Labour leader in the United Kingdom is called one.

Centralization is a Marxist plan. As a result of central banks, perpetraitors have stolen millions individually in usury on governments, companies, and our brothers and sisters. It was Alexander Hamilton who wanted one in this nation and Jefferson's party fought him bitterly, for this is another step to a government of absolutism. Of course, the centralized bank expanded its power and has coined all of its money without it being on the gold standard, which is expressly un-Constitutional. Educators of history teach that the government would have been impotent without a Federal bank, but again it is un-Constitutional. People have been becoming rich from the interest the taxed pay just to have a currency due to the Federal Reserve. This hampers every trade, while it is argued that loans at interest stimulate economic growth. When one looks at everything on a large scale, this only aids the borrower initially, whereas an enormous portion of the GDP goes to paying usurers that produce nothing. Most cannot crawl out of the depths of debt and the bank gets their collateral as surety, thereby decreasing their risk. The wealth of anyone who pays interest is decreased usually unless they use it for investment. Usury is immoral and obnoxious that is why it was forbidden for Christians for centuries.

Furthermore, the government is a strain on the economy for not producing anything and with its fines there should be more lenity. The amount owed for fines has been desolating those who are guilty. The Sixth and Eighth Amendments guarantee one to a speedy trial by which one may be faced by the accuser, prohibits cruel and unusual punishment, and forbids excessive fines. Notwithstanding these rights, the government actually advertises the fact that a DUI costs ten thousand dollars and as far as affordability to a majority of people this is excessive however punitive it is meant to be. This places the offender in servitude to the government, solely, for months of labor.

The only defense for this is public safety, but the perpetraitors have an ulterior motive. They know that the spirit of Liberty prior to the Revolution began in the taverns and if they can prevent people from socializing when they tend to really speak their minds, they will do so. The excessive fines prevent most people from going to the bar who need a car for transportation and are subversive to our freedom to assemble. These laws are draconian, most people at bars behave like any sober person way beyond the limit of .08. Conservatism does not reflect this opinion entirely because in the South its opinions actually result in dry counties. This country desperately needs for most things to be decided on the county level as specified by the Bill of Rights. The Tenth Amendment has pronounced that most powers would be left up to the States or the people and the counties represent the "people" as do the municipality governments. How else would the "people" be categorized, unless the current perpetraitor's doctrine is that the "people" means the Federal government with all of its encroachments upon States' rights? It is obvious that the separate States were to have sovereignty and the argument that the "people" represented anything but a lesser grouping of representation is flimsy, at best. The capacity possessed by the Federal government to rule justly was highly in doubt by the Framers of our Constitution and that is why it was to be limited.

Everything almost is made overseas, especially in Communist China for easier profits, it is said. It is hard to compete with the starving Chinese when it comes to wages, but without proof, the author is free to speculate that something is awry. First of all, we are not obliged to them for making products we purchase, there is a huge trade deficit between us, and they are putting Americans out of work. Could this be a way to bleed the United States dry and who gave the instructions to let this happen? In light of what has been demonstrated in this text, this should be seen as another example of the Communist conspiracy for world domination and how the perpetraitor forsakes our country. This deficit needs to be reversed and tariffs look like the only answer since it is more expensive to manufacture products here with the benefits and higher wages. America is the last vestige of freedom in the world and this is yet another way the Communists are trying to takeover. One of their goals more than a half of a century ago was to have us practice free trade with China, so that they could make a fortune.

The Leftists are basically traitors to the United States of America. They come from all walks of life from the poorest to the richest who live in extravagance with one thing in common, they have been corrupted with Liberal ideology. Trump likes to point out that some of them are the Hollywood elite who lack fidelity to their country. Everyone knows that actors are eccentric, to say the least, but their expectations are that no one protest their unwholesome filth they place on the silver screen. That is one reason for their rift with the moral majority that sees through all of their pomp and red carpets. Hollywood is responsible for conquering a large portion of public opinion for the Democrats because people see fame with all of the emotions of envy wrapped around it and think that if an actor supports an issue, then it is right. However illogical that sounds, beauty and popularity play a huge role in this and expect for more famous people to become politicians because name recognition is the number one goal of well-financed campaigns. Movies incite passion and are instrumental in formulating public opinion about the topics they address. Films can shape our perceptions by portraying a certain type of person as good or bad and people have learned way too many falsities from them. In fact, persuasion is the motive for many writers and the plot, characters, and themes are all just tools to make a person agree with them. Only, it is common knowledge that these influential people are distinguished for their radical Liberalism. They are actively conspiring to alter political view-points, in fact, the first full length motion picture is credited for reviving the Ku Klux Klan because it showed them in a heroic manner.

How does radical Muslim terror come into play with the schemes of the Perpe-traitors? The Muslim terrorists are so resolute in their hatred because of their beliefs of Muhammad who taught that Islam must be spread by the sword. It is no trivial fact in history that they have been against Christians because of the Crusades. Also, there seems to be a correlation between Black Power, Communism, and Islam and in Africa they are placing confidence in all three after breaking off the yoke of Christian colonialism. The terrorists are proceeding like the Leftists did over a century ago here in America and because she is the enemy of Communism, the Muslim terrorists are its allies in that they have a common enemy. Not surprisingly, the Left has expressed disapproval for many of the elements of the War on Terror. They would honestly rather hear of a white man being the culprit of the next act of terrorism than a Muslim. The reason for this is that they want to force acceptance of Muslims; tolerance of all is the key to Communism. To them, the rich Capitalist will continue to tread upon the interests of the proletariat as long as he is divided racially. History is told by the victors and there is a long list of nations that have turned Socialist, Communist, or Muslim over the last century compared to few who have newly embraced the opposite. So be prepared for a multitude of immigrants into any country of European descent like Muslims, and for terrorism and crime to increase in these places. The bulk of the opposition to Communism came from the West and it is currently being strategically invaded to pressure us into a loss now that we gave into Socialism. They are scrambling over to areas of income redistribution to soak it up like a sponge while demoralizing us with acts of terror. This asserted effort by these perpe-traitors is characteristic of nothing that has ever occurred in the history of mankind. It is again unprecedented, the Soviet Union fell, but the threat is not over, nor is the opposition desperate. Their global tactics have shifted and terrorism is being used as ammunition against the remnants of Capitalism. The terrorists show no loyalty to one idea, but are the result of pure evil. Sometimes it is a bomb, a plane, a knife, or mass shooting; all in all, we are displaying the inadequacies of gun control. In comparison to Israel, where many people walk around with automatic weapons because of Muslim terror attacks, we are utterly defenseless. The answer is to allow without a permit, the open carry of a weapon, not the confiscation of all guns.

Of course, these perpetraitors have continued to raise taxes on cigarettes under the excuse that it will prevent people from smoking. In reality, it is keeping people in poverty or they are quitting and replacing it with medication for anxiety, depression, etc.

Meantime, they are legalizing marijuana which is worse than tobacco and the perpetraitors know that pot hardly ever causes people to become more conservative. The debate in America between Liberalism and Conservatism might be decided once millions of more people get high and "open their minds" to Liberal delusions. Also, smoking helped our economy because tobacco is the number one cash crop. Now the government is trampling all over these profits and wrecking American interests with a Communist motive, no doubt. Their excuse for this contrivance against our freedom to smoke; it is that the government ends up paying for many people who get diseases from cigarettes later in life? Expect the government to have ushered in many other controls over our private lives after they have decided to pay for even more aspects of it. Just understand that none of this has happened accidentally, it is all part of a concerted effort to manipulate us strictly to obey the perpe-traitors in our government.

As the author was writing, the President has become impeached due to the sheer obstinacy of the Democrats who know there

is no chance he will be convicted in the
Senate. The House Speaker claimed that she
would not impeach unless there was
bipartisan support and yet she led this
mischief with only Democrats (a few even
defected). The Democratic majority-led
House was still victorious even though the
Constitution states that a President must be
guilty of high crimes or misdemeanors. The
preponderance of evidence shows that he
has done nothing illegal and that the Perpe-
Traitors yet again have loosely interpreted
the Constitution and used impeachment for
political reasons. The President is everyone
in America's superior and to try to oust the
leader of the Free World is like a coup de'
tat. They are to the Constitution as heretics
are to the church. The Democrats could not
impeach him for being a skeptic of global
warming, for his hard stance on illegal
immigration, etc., so they just acted like he
did something unlawful. This is just another
of the calamities our country now must
endure because of these Liberal
perpetraitors. This will weaken the
President's ability to work internationally
for the benefit of our people.

Impeaching the President was also a campaign strategy for defeating his attempt at re-election. This judgment reflects the unparalleled hatred Democrats have for Donald Trump. It also reflects how bitter they were to lose the election of 2016 and it is their attempt to over-turn it. The masses are divided with most of the people who voted against him supporting impeachment. The polls out have recently changed and show that he is now leading against all of his opponents and some say it is because the impeachment was so political. Trump and his party invested in the economy with large tax-cuts and it looks like it is paying off. Contrary to what is taught by the Liberals, Keynesian economics is nothing compared to Reaganomics and the polls may be displaying him favored because of this, too. Trump is also a great speaker due to his charisma, though he is not necessarily eloquently using a high vocabulary. He has been in business and knows to keep things simple and connects with the audience, which leaves the Democrats miserable. In politics he is pursuing issues that people really have feelings for and has managed to keep his base beside him with their full support. So the grassroots of the Republican

Party is satisfied with him and that is why
the Senators are happy to oppose his
conviction over the supposed impeachable
offenses. Most of the issues he has decided
to act on or support have demonstrated that
Trump is a real blessing upon America.
Despite all of the unfairness in the media, he
is still on top. President Trump is ready to
defend this magnificent country as
Commander-in-Chief, as well. He has led us
into the prosperity that God has intended for
us. These are the real reasons the perpetraitors have chosen to impeach our leader.
If he had been a Democrat and someone
who did not deviate from Liberalism, this
would have never happened.

Chapter X

The Puritans started this nation and
preached that we were to be a City Upon a
Hill, a light to the world. Our Founders were
virtuous and knew that their work and that
of their posterity would be the hope of all
men, created equal. We were not meant to
live in communes, the Pilgrims tried this

experiment and it failed very quickly. They had reform and sided with private ownership of the land in the New World. The Pilgrims found that people would not work without a monetary incentive and the nation was not founded by strikers who could not be lawfully fired. Most of the things Liberals stand for are not ancient rights, but have all come about after the "Communist Manifesto". The purpose of the impeachment process was to ensure that the President did not get away with criminal activity. The author is entirely convinced that the entire government is guilty of an abuse of power; look at what happened at Waco. Clinton should have had the Attorney General, Janet Reno, fired for that without hesitation. As the compound at Waco burned, people thought of their right to assemble and bear arms when they witnessed on television this real abuse of power. If anything, Trump's innocuous phone call to Ukraine was his freedom of speech. The Democrats are definitely not holding back, but have been endlessly investigating him with a mind for impeachment from the day he was sworn into office.

As was mentioned previously, perpetraitors are burning the American Flag and the Liberal courts have ruled that is the freedom of expression. The tradition is to respect it, especially for the sake of our Armed Forces, but hypocritically the Left saw no problem giving a man sixteen years in prison for burning a gay pride flag. He got more time than just what he would have received for a misdemeanor theft because he supposedly "hated" homosexuals. Why are the Liberals so occupied with protecting a bad flag, but not a good flag? Well, it is pretty clear from what the author has been saying in this book. There is a clear double standard in this case where the man was protesting using his First Amendment right and where the American Flag burner cannot be charged with arson like he was. This is all because Obama decided to pass a "Hate Crime" bill which most took to mean it would apply to those who commit racial violence. This legislation has gone international and when a man who had a sex-change was a denied a pornographic role in England, they began investigating it as a hate crime! Obviously, the law's detractors were right when they objected to what exactly would be constituted a hate crime and that there is hatred when any races are involved in violence illegally, already.

Also, this acceptance of homosexuality has somehow been related to racial tolerance. Blacks identify with homosexuals as yet another minority-segment of the population treated differently with memories of racial injustice. Only, being gay involves an immoral sexual act, whereas being black is something a person cannot change. There are all of these arguments now, put forward at first by the homosexuals themselves that they should not go to hell because they were born that way or that it is impossible to change. The perpetraitors have created a myth in order to make it normal and not queer to have sex with the same gender. They have accomplished their efforts rapidly and unfortunately we have to allow them to serve in our military alongside women which did not make us any stronger necessarily. There was no overwhelming necessity for them to serve and it caused a lack of morale and controversy amongst believers of all faiths. Having women in a masculine role of combat is what the Communists did and look, according to the Liberals, we should be more like them.

Equality-minded feminists were claiming they should be able to walk around top-less in public because men could and the courts upheld this notion. Due to the excuses of equality in Colorado and many other states it is illegal to stop a woman from exposing her naked breasts, now. At the same time, feminists claim that if women were elected there would be no more armed conflicts because men are more warlike. The way to respect women in this country is to afford them protection, not offer them a rifle and tell them to attack a foe. That is the traditional way war has been practiced by all cultures probably because women mostly used to be pregnant or nursing at young adulthood. Women usually are incapable of passing the basic training requirements of men, so they lower the standards for them which is a paradox for equality. People that are oppressed by political correctness would be reluctant to point out that all of our great military victories have been won by men. Liberals have made it ordinary for women and gays to be in the military and yet are still the ones who say that its members are not respectable, what hypocrisy, especially since they only mean the straight male ones!

The Republicans are more practical when it comes to issues than the Democrats. The legislation they implement is more beneficial for the whole population, not just those who receive aid from the Federal government. Each side displays themselves as instruments of change which is appealing to those voters who know the system is broken, but do not understand why. To some moderates who have not taken enough stands on the issues, the presentation by the candidates is everything. Everyone recognizes certain standards that should be upheld, no matter what side of the aisle, like being fair. Only, that is a notion that is perceived differently to all, for example, Communists believe that profits ought to be shared equally with the workers. To them this is the remedy to economic disparity, whereas American Capitalists believe that no remedy is needed and that the risk of investing in a business is enough justification for high returns. Notice that the Democrats resemble the Communists more, according to them income inequality is a problem. The government's ability to create and run businesses is what the radical Left does not doubt, whereas the Right-wing realizes that our government is limited and businesses should be left to how they form under natural conditions.

The inequality of wages is the motivation behind the laws on the minimum wage. If this was really a good thing, why would not the Republicans be for it because it clearly would make them more popular? They are being accused now of racial hatred for not supporting its increase because minorities disproportionately work at a minimum wage. In fact, they are bold to stand up for what is right even though it may not appear to be so on the face of it. The minimum wage actually does stretch the ability for small businesses to pay their workers. It is also correct to assert that a rise in wages artificially, results in job loss. The Republicans show that they have true insight on this issue because it causes inflation. Looking deeper into the wage gap and minimum wage, one will discover that the more money people have overall, the more products will increase in price. This is the result of inflation and a rise in wages; economic growth goes down because of it. Inflation is like a regressive tax on the people. In Illinois, the minimum wage increased by almost twice as much and those rewarded with it will benefit if they can manage to have a position still, but the wants of this small minority of people end up wreaking havoc on the majority in this country.

The Leftists are blameworthy when it comes to Big Government Socialism. It is difficult to foresee how this can be reconciled with our Constitution's vision of a limited government. They have little faith in the great philanthropies organized to aid fellow man and if taxes were lowered, more people could donate and tithe. The Leftists have bashed prayer as a reaction to the mass shootings, thinking they can take things into their own hands by banning guns. They have lost all confidence in businesses' ability to treat people fairly without the government's intervention. In theory, with representation we should suffer less oppression than from a dictator, but a monarchy has the potential to protect property just as much as a democracy; it all depends if the people are led by morals or avarice. The expenses are so high for the government to administer laws because there are so many workers involved in their execution. The government needs to be streamlined the way that profitable businesses are. The Left has become downright scornful of Trump supporters publicly with numerous assaults and degrading insults because they are deluded. Howbeit, the Right-wing is actually on track to seize complete control of the Supreme Court, allowing for the reversal of Roe v. Wade. When this society fails to protect innocent life, it has failed the ideals spoken of in the Declaration of Independence; "life, liberty, and the pursuit of happiness".

This is not to say that the Republicans are innocent; there are easily a thousand elected ones that could be considered perpetraitors. We really needed the President to step up against government excess, had he have vetoed the omnibus spending bill that increased domestic spending by billions, the country would be in much better shape. It seems that Republicans that would like to sincerely decrease spending are fewer and that they really are just for a smaller increase in spending than the Democrats. No one has been literally traduced in this work because the facts stand for themselves. More people who take the time to read things like this will believe in the real truth of the matter

and thus mud-slinging is not necessary;
informed people are naturally more loyal.
Bias is detected when facts are presented
that are meant to decrease one's love of
country and the fundamentals of citizenship.
The increase in domestic spending was a
concession by the Republicans to find
support for an increase in military spending.
What we do not need is a huge standing
army, which is the bane of freedom, and
infantry is almost as outdated as the cavalry
when compared to tanks, jet-fighters,
nuclear submarines, and bombs. We could
destroy an entire civilization with just our
Air Force; there will no longer be thousands
of soldiers lined up in a row opposed by a
similar army. Automatics have made such
an advance almost suicide and guerilla
warfare like in Vietnam is more likely than
the type of battles that took place in the
World Wars before atomic weapons. The
need for a military that is as vigorous as
today's which has never been stronger, is
debatable. One should emphasize the fact
that America is not at war technically and
has no intention of invading another nation
when opposing the massive military budget.

Elected officials should be constantly trying to find improvements to the existing laws to save money, not creating new laws. The principal laws began with the Mosaic ones and then the Common Law which King Alfred codified using the former. The first set of important ones were the Body of Liberties, in 17th century Massachusetts, which if interpreted correctly would mean all debts would be relinquished after fifty years. Even though the laws were consistent for many centuries, today's laws would be incompatible with the Bible's. The eternal Lord gave us them, but now they are so neglected and rejected by mankind who believe they know better than their own Creator. There are many religious imitators who are after the offering plate, but do not support the inerrant Word of God! God's law is imperishable, though some believe only the Jews need to follow the Old Testament, but Jesus said He was here to fulfill it. No one for over two thousand years supposed that the principal laws were not to be followed, but it is true that in order to be considered a Christian only four of them must be followed according to Paul and that all things to eat are now clean. This information is mentioned to demonstrate how far man has thought to rebel with new and endless statutes and that we are not just changing our ancestors' decisions, but God's.

So whose scheme is it exactly out of all of these perpe-traitors, Karl Marx? With proper reasoning, one may discover that at the base of it all is Satan. This is my conviction because of all of the deaths surrounding Communist governments, the satanic abortion of millions of American babies, and the sexual revolution where our culture has been turned up-side down from what God intended. Any reversal of the current trends would just be postponing the inevitable. After the separation of the Ten Tribes of Israel from Judah who rebelled because of high taxes, both kingdoms of God's chosen people began a downward spiral of morals that resulted in them being conquered and massively deported. Our country is also strangled by vexatious regulations, taxes, and immorality, so how will this outcome be any different? This history of the Israelites is indelible however much the Leftists would like to do so by banning the truth from our public schools. The author is insinuating that something like this might happen to

America and that similar perpe-traitors were at work in Israel with like tactics. They may have faced the same threats as we did in a broad sense like how they would burn their children as sacrifices to Moloch similar to how we are practicing abortions on a large scale. One might be under the impression that to Satan both of these types of innocent killings are equally satisfying to him, if one is able to put two and two together. Satan is working extremely methodically with subtle changes in our media that look to be almost ridiculous in retrospect. To say that Satan alone bears the responsibility would be to ignore all of his enablers. They have turned the film industry into an abomination and the Bible warns that we are to keep evil from our eyes. There is no placating these perpe-traitors who are being orchestrated by Satan to behave as puppets.

Even though America hears two conflicting voices from the Right and the Left, the answer is clear. It is hard to navigate through all of the hogwash of the Leftist media and their strategy to rule it has served them well. After continuously disseminating facts convenient to their version of reality, they have made progress

with the voter. They have profaned the Bible
and by doing so are in direct service to
Satan. They have made a mockery of
Christianity, not for their instantaneous
amusement, but to destroy faith because
atheism is fundamental to Communist
ideology. Confidence in our government can
only be restored once these perpe-traitors
who are aiding and abetting our enemies are
exposed and brought to justice. The only
way our Constitution can be restored is if
Conservatives have seized control of our
government, ousting the Liberals, and then
they must prevent them from returning to
power. We must not be plunged into armed
conflict when the gun control debate comes
to a head or the public will be plagued with
misinformation, branding us as terrorists. It
is doubtful that the government will refrain
from being even more tyrannical in such a
situation. Insubordination to restrictive gun
laws yes, but not a civil war which would
only make us more susceptible to foreign
threats and might even give the perpetraitors an opportunity to revolt in favor of
Communism. Incompetent Liberals are
already labelling the National Rifle
Association a terrorist organization. The
Left has depended on gradualness for over a

century and to say they only want to go after assault weapons without suspecting more would be naïve. Also, the perpe-traitor led military and law enforcement do not want to face the menace of a semi-automatic weapon because they are expecting the possibility of revolt. Patriots of this country are already at an extreme disadvantage if they are ever called upon to dissolve the government by force and the elites want to keep things as unfair as possible. The author is one of the descendants of a man who believed in armed rebellion for freedom and practiced it. It is mighty curious how our people enjoy the benefits of this idea without the backbone to enforce it or even to provide for the means to do so.

The people are spoiled with luxuries that the Revolutionary soldiers could never imagine and yet liberty was defended still. Would the perpe-traitors have called George Washington a schizophrenic and done away with him because of his hallucinations at Valley Forge where an angel visited him and foretold the future? Yes, but he defended his valor and became the first President of the United States of America. We have inherited this country from the soldiers of the

Revolutionary War, but almost no one can recall the name of even one of them besides the guy who told them to shoot up the government's military. The people who claim he was not a Christian act as though they are illiterate because he was known to pray often, kept a prayer journal, and wrote about the tenets of it and Jesus Christ. Liberty is the key to America's longevity, but people just do not seem to have that same spirit of '76. Freedom was the dream that they all fought for. In comparison to them our people are apathetic towards the notion and bordering on pathetic.

Now they are telling adult individuals under 21 that they can fight for their country, but not have a drink or a cigarette. Not to be redundant, but a child cannot have wine at Communion, but can over-rule his parents and Maker regarding his own gender. The officious government can now effectively sterilize your child against your will with sex-changing hormones because of the success of the radical homosexual agenda. The author has made a deliberate effort to make Leftists look horrible and to make the reader mad about it. Witness Christ's persecution at Christmas time.

Notice how everyone now knows that materialism is bad, has more of it than ever, and really its opposition is not spiritually minded, but rather another vehicle of hatred against Capitalism. Our American culture languishes under the yoke of multi-culturalism as though we would not get along with other races unless we are presented with more books by other cultures than our own. It is fine to learn about other people within the confines of our own ethno-centric perspective, but now we are overburdened by it. This indoctrination includes vaulting shame and injecting us with false guilt if we like our culture better. I think our country peaked before we were told there is no right or wrong answer, other cultures are just different not better or worse, there are no winners or losers, etc. Without the acknowledged existence of absolute truths, intellectual persuasion becomes brainwashing. Leftist machinations involve confusing a subject with moral relativism to destroy what one believes, thereby opening their mind to change. An appropriate response to hearing what is not true might be anger if one does not play along, but that makes one susceptible to authoritarian punishments.

So what attributes must a person possess to meet the criteria of being a perpetraitor? Definitely atheists are, whose religion is evolution and oppose any mention of God in the name of science. They vastly contribute to our people's moral decline, however much they argue otherwise, in a boundless way. Anyone who imposes Liberalism upon their audience in a manner that supposes they are in-erring in an effort to persuade regular people into accepting Leftist teachings. Without the philosophical consent of the people, their progress will ultimately fail and the desire to present facts or educate is not what compels a perpetraitor, but rather they are driven by a will to affect a change in public opinion. Also, they are cowards that hide behind pacifism in an effort to avoid fighting in wars and will not even work. One must differentiate between good and bad ones, but bankers, politicians, lawyers, and psychologists who are unethical should be included. Race and labor agitators that raise discontent to the point of madness are also some. Criminals who would weaken us through drug use also lack virtue like the PerpeTraitors. Radical environmentalists that show contempt for modern civilization that take conservation efforts too far are some. People who generally lack moral discipline, sinners, who cause much evil to the detriment of America are perpetraitors. Globalists who wish to consolidate all the separate nations into one are. Members of the Communist Party, its sympathizers, the Socialist Party, the Green Party, and Antifa (who is under the Department of Homeland Security's suspicion as being a terrorist organization) are perpetraitors, as well. You simply have to draw the line in the sand somewhere, but the list goes on and on.

Chapter XI

The leaders of the Democratic Party are also the quintessential perpetraitors. The Constitutional relevance of anything they have attempted to change is non-existent. Politically, they are not for a limited government unless it means silencing religious expression of anything state-funded. Now that their leaders have been insulted, it should also be said that their followers are guilty of various false beliefs.

This is usually where they make an effort to play a little game by stating there are no right or wrong opinions, but hypocritically they will turn around and say what we believe is false to their allies. An alternative opinion may be more tolerated by them, but at least we do not pretend that all opinions are of equal value. They do this to shock their victim and to portray them as a dunce while simultaneously getting more listeners aboard the crazy train of their humanistic religion. Now these Liberal professors need only to be capable of mustering their pupils to vote Democrat in order to gain control of the entire country, so see how it begins with a small amount of influential people. The potential is enormous with this method for within a generation all public school teachers were under the thumb of Liberal professors. This is indispensable for the Left and the college students are no longer taught to focus on names and dates in the study of history, but are graded by a more subjective manner. Students are impelled to describe history in terms of a Marxist perspective and the professors will act like you do not make any sense while using plain English if it does not support something Leftist. The consequence of bribing the establishment with tuition is an avoidance of manual labor, but I felt like I was selling my soul, personally. It is like an intellectual apprenticeship from the dark side and the majority is forced to conform to silence on religion because other paying students are Jews or Muslims. With faith the fundamentals of each religion are very similar, but how come they do not have to tolerate us?

Often the Democrats are inflexible when it comes to compromise. Practically every time a Republican executive, whether it be a governor or president, defies their spending increases amidst humongous debt by veto or refusal to sign, the Republican is accused of shutting down the government. Every year Conservatives who want deep cuts in the budget are disappointed. Certainly, the Republican executive would not hesitate to fund over ninety-five percent of what is asked for, but the Democrats will not compromise and always ask for way more than is needed as a bargaining tactic in anticipation of proposals to cut the budget. Picture oneself in an observatory, viewing an asteroid heading for Earth. That is what it is like for America with this amount of overspending. We are heading for sudden disaster one way or the other and the Democrats are not merely ignorant, they are purposely perpetrating this country's demise. They do not simply forget that we have to pay a staggering amount of interest on these debts; they are actually traitors hoping to bleed us dry. Even without the unfunded liabilities which are more than twice the debt, the principal owed is not even reasonable and would never be offered in proportion to income privately unless the strategy is to own all the collateral. This shows how wrong they are to use their absolute power to bury us in debt in order to sell-out our country. There need not even be any civil disturbances or revolts for America to become foreign owned. These politicians' odious actions in public reflect all the dirt our adversaries must have on them, for politics is one scandal after another and to think spies and foreign interests have nothing to do with these perpetraitors would be misleading, at best. This is why it is so important that they be defeated. We may boast all we would like about our ideals, but slavery to interest and debts is not freedom.

Our global service economy is like a
harlot that provides instant gratification
while producing nothing except maybe a
bastard of usury. The pain that Uncle Sam
endures because of these PerpeTraitors is
excruciating. The international banking
interests will have us reduced to less than
peasants because at least they have work and
now there is an epidemic of homelessness
with tent cities, filth, etc. It is difficult for
even a landlord to make money these days
with all of the credit card interest payments
tenants have to pay across the board. Some
Socialists are now making matters worse by
artificially imposing rent control on what
they consider tribute to a landlord. This is
just another notion they have developed that
shows favoritism to the poor that creates
havoc. These people think they are heroic
for protesting against rent when the free
market should decide its cost. The Left
needs to be scrutinized for supporting caps
on rent because they are ambivalent to the
fact that they are forcing the landlord to
provide them with a place to live for
nothing. Without profit, this is exploitation
of the property owner who needs a return in
order to just meet the requirements of
maintenance and taxes, hardly being able to

break even. This would be
counterproductive to the market and
landlords are being treated as though they
should be like rich benefactors to complete
strangers or something. This is not to say
that people are not suffering from high rent,
but that the issue parallels all the others the
perpetraitors are behind. Admittedly, there is
a lot of tension between tenants and
landlords, but each should be thankful for
the other. Oftentimes, real estate investors
are just hoping for a margin of the return
that the banks get, having borrowed from
them money at a certain percentage perhaps,
so the high prices are a result of the financial
system. In the end, this will be to no avail to
those who rent because less property will be
developed or available as a result of
artificial rent controls. These Socialistic
suggestions will only result in more
government ownership of property, like
subsidized housing, where everyone is
crammed into small areas within drab
complexes. Decipher the issue properly and
one will find that this is what the
Communist wants. By the way, it is not an
aspiration of the local bank to carry on the
duties of the landlord, so we cannot have
this middle man cut out of the picture to

reduce rent which will happen if the government forces them to lower rents below profitability.

All these perpetraitors ever do is diminish the potential of our people. The amount of investments in job producing companies would be countless more if less of America's disposable income went to taxes. This is an argument that those who should be showing solidarity for Capitalism need to utilize. Even though George W. Bush conquered Iraq, he was still not able to implement the privatization of Social Security to save it because people thought it too risky. The program cannot survive endlessly at this rate and will be insolvent very soon which is more of a risk than to do nothing to fix or reform it. The moment privatization of the Social Security behemoth takes place, if it ever does, participants will get to use their portion of taxes owed to invest in business allowing them more potential benefits than what the government currently offers. He also advocated this because it would grow the Gross Domestic Product eventually, instead of having the money wasted or stagnant and suffering from inflation. It all adds up and

the people's bank accounts would increase.
These Liberal entitlements are the most
expensive part of our government and the
situation is desperate. If the stock market
flattened out or crashed, the investments
would only be allowed to be made
conservatively under his plan, anyways. The
only ploy the Left has to bail out FDR's
Social Security is to raise taxes even higher.

These perpetraitors live with impunity
conducting their campaigns for "progress"
in their various stages. Their persistency
means that the law will not stand in the way
and they are protected by the Democratic
Party. The reason why over ten candidates
were fielded for President was to keep the
fire away from one man, thereby sharing the
heat of accusations or else if only a few they
would be unprotected. There is safety in
numbers and they want everyone talking the
same thing in a herd-like mentality. They are
still clinging to the hope that they can defeat
Trump, so if one falls from scandal another
can pick up from where he left off to
continue the race. Really, they should all be
ashamed of themselves for standing up there
and supporting these disastrous policies. To
memory, the only good thing came from

Bernie Sanders who wants to lower the caps on the amount of interest the credit card companies can charge. Millions of Americans are struggling with credit card payments and yet those rates should be left to the States to decide unless we want an autocracy. The King of France succeeded in lowering the cap on all interest to help the economy centuries ago, so there is nothing new under the sun.

Pretty soon the government will be promising you cures for diseases in an effort to buy your allegiance and people will put up with so much more because they are desperate. The disintegration of our limited government has arisen slowly, since its conception. After each disruption of our Constitutional law, the Left has been saying things are getting better while the Right says things are getting worse. There has been a replacement of our faith in God with a false belief in secular humanism. Public safety has become paramount to personal liberty. It is true that the standard of living has become comparatively higher for all since the Revolution due to an increase in technology, but the government from Washington created almost none of these advances, so that is irrelevant. A true illumination of the circumstances: people gave their lives for inalienable rights on the battle-field and now one's health or longevity in old age is too important to resist Socialism. People still have the opportunity to reject the government's complete overthrow of private health-care, but they have different priorities. It should be considered that once it is free, more people will undergo expensive and previously unattainable medical solutions, but they keep saying less will be spent overall, which is a lie. Wearisome to Christians who oppose sex-changes, these operations will come to be considered a right, they will increase due to government funding, and society will even pressure men who are too masculine to partake in these so-called treatments to lower the population. Once the government has to spend a half a million on each citizen, it will be considered pragmatic to reduce the population and it will be necessitated through abortion, euthanasia, sterilization, sex-changes, and the conversions to homosexuality recommended by doctors all through Washington, D.C. Evidently, people do not know about the positions that professionals have taken on these issues and

the psychological establishment has all sorts
of untraditional views now of gender that
insist that it is a problem even against the
patient's will. They promote their theories as
science while admitting that the founder of
their branch of study was completely wrong
about everything indicating that something
is up with it. Humanity is now viewed in a
hypochondriac fashion where everyone has
something wrong with them, so that money
is owed to professionals who are ready to
lay down excuses for misbehavior that is
confronted by the police state with
compulsory medication. A person may
undergo a traumatic experience and then be
utterly led on by the establishment to
become dependent on them as a victim. The
force behind psychology is atheism where
they will compare human activity to animal
test subjects' and draw conclusions
accordingly. Its position in science is really
just a manifestation of authority and one that
supplies the government with surveillance,
assuming that the patient is diagnosed with
this or that, they may have reason to believe
that they should be controlled because they
might do something like somebody else.
Each new claim they make has nothing to do
with freedom, but rather control and it

demonstrates how afraid or paranoid the people have become of their fellow man. The misconceptions about the mentally ill are perpetuated by the media and actually the worse kind, the schizophrenic, is more likely to be the victim of violence than a perpetrator of it.

This gradual march of so-called progress by the perpetraitors has only been delayed by the Conservatives, historically. For example, Conservatives were able to stop the world governance of the League of Nations because it was a violation of our national sovereignty. This effort was transferred into the United Nations which they were no longer able to postpone. Subsequently, the rise of homosexuality was another gradual process. At first, sodomy was banned in States across the Union and in Ireland until 1983, but slowly it went from being illegal to simply a moral question. Of course, now we are dealing with state sanctioned acceptance like marriage, anti-discrimination laws, and even the church must be led by openly gay ministers according to them. Another march of progress has been women's suffrage, then their removal from the homes to places of employment, their phony right to abortions, and then finally they are led into combat with machine guns. Is this legitimate progress or a regression? None of this has been exaggerated, weakening the patriarchal system and the family unit is a sure way to corrode a civilization.

It is clear that we must choose the direction we are to take before our rights disappear. Even the fact that we are able to choose our course may eventually be usurped if our right to bear arms is not kept. The American dream is becoming more difficult to attain than ever with all of the immigrants competing for our jobs and the global competition. The materials our possessions are made of are of less value if one compares antiques to the chinsy products of today. The future is coming and history has proven that religion can be very resilient. It has been a long time since we have stoned adulterers to death, but it is still illegal although there is no punishment. Could it be that our ancestors lived with it complacently or that it was too difficult or prevalent to punish? The Left wants us to learn lessons from history like, "oh look at what the Puritans used to do with the scarlet letter, do not ever let it happen again"! I am not against interest being cultivated about history, but please realize that everything taught about it is now in the context of a liberation from morality, the church, your own dad, your own right to exist in the environment, and this cannot last. We still have not succumbed to idolatry because there is not temptation from the Devil to create any unfamiliar statues, besides Mary's and Buddha's or the television. His determination to subvert God's plan has been adequately met through atheism and general doubt about the supernatural. This may not even be suitable to say because it is so obvious, but God is definitely not for the minion perpetraitors.

So what's good, otherwise? Certainly, American capital punishment is good. After a just trial, which I believe should have at least two witnesses in order to sentence a person to death, capital punishment for murder is eventually administered. Thankfully, this has been the law since the dawn of time in order to execute the monster who spills innocent blood. Of course, God's enemies have been against it like everything else that is good even misconstruing one of the Ten Commandments, "Thou shalt not kill". It does not take a genius to logically determine that the death penalty for violent murder does not contradict God's law because He instituted the practice in the book of Genesis over two thousand years before Moses reaffirmed it in the Pentateuch. It is terrifying that someone would argue this anyways as though the penalty for "Thou shalt not kill" was not death or that it applies to livestock, too. Even John Wesley, the founder of the Methodists, would rebuke this false reasoning, though he abstained from meat and the denomination, by the way, is now against capital punishment. The excuses are not to be tolerated like oh, he was insane, drunk, or wrongly convicted due to a technicality. Anyone who rules for life in prison after the accused has been witnessed murdering by two people, at least, is ignoring how the earth itself cries out for justice after being soaked with blood and has a devil-may-care attitude. It can also be argued that punishments like this are deterrents to future homicidal people and once they are executed, they will not get to act in such a bloodthirsty way again.

The PerpeTraitors must be exposed to help the plight of millions of Americans. We must restore the institutions of this great country that have fallen under the control of the Left. They have infiltrated every profession and are working to destroy free-enterprise. They have not appreciated the loyalty of our soldiers in fighting for their country and portray veterans as crazed victims from the horrors of war. The author here is not being pitiless, he sympathizes with the veteran who in some instances even becomes homeless because real masculinity is somehow seen as unbecoming of service sector positions. Because of the Left's intolerance of them and middle-aged, straight white guys, they are not able to live up to the expectations of all of their customers like cheery women and gays. Much of our resources are expended on veterans which is not wrong by any means, but again this only indirectly applies to our defense, so the individual States should have the right to take care of them. The Federal government must learn to be submissive to States' rights and allow them to raise their taxes by lowering its own immensely. It is uncanny how often the Ninth and Tenth Amendments have been thwarted, disregarded, and forgotten basically as being inalienable rights of Americans. The author is tolerant of all races, religions, and homosexuals, so this reasoning is not code for bringing back segregation or slavery and is frustrated that that is the stigma attached to States' Rights. Why go through all the trouble of having fifty State governments that do little in comparison to the national one; it seems like a waste since the Perpetraitors have centralized everything according to Communist beliefs and the courts have things rigged, so that States may only differ from Federal laws if they have a Liberal ambition, mostly?

Paralyzed with debt and encumbered by an ever increasing centralized government, the perpe-traitors have us right where they want. They no longer have to rely on their fellow comrade to report their neighbor, for the technology for surveillance is of a great magnitude. Expect the police state to start accumulating dossiers on everyone, not just criminals or terrorist suspects. There will be statutes allowing for information gathering on racists, at first, then anyone suspected of intolerance to guard against hate crimes, and finally gun owners. A list of everything from one's salary to one's family will go into a single file along with any psychoanalysis leading to a diagnosis from a government paid professional. Job applications will include the availability of their contents to the government file to see if you are lying about prior convictions. They will find out from entries on social media what you should be suspected of according to statistical methods and believe it or not, if you are poor all of this information may already be monitored just not consolidated into one source. For example, the tedious data gathering is held from the list above from the following Federal agencies, respectively; the Internal Revenue Service, the United States Census Bureau, the Social Security Administration, the Department of Housing and Urban Development, the Federal Bureau of Investigation, and the Department of Homeland Security. The last two would apply to suspected criminals and terrorists currently until the politicians make a pact with the Devil over the pragmatism of holding information on everyone like in China. If you really want a civil servant to spy on you, go ahead and praise the future further centralization for it will support you for free from cradle to grave, unless you are

employed by it directly. It already is a
snatcher of children, if you are opposed to
vaccinations, support corporal punishment,
are addicted to a substance, or are diagnosed
with something that has to do with any of
your mental faculties, which includes
probably half the population. They have not
wrested the children from all of these
mothers because there are not enough
comrades to report to the social workers yet,
but wait until the cameras enter into your
home or you are tracked using biometric
data or a chip.

Chapter XII

The perpetraitors also started the trend
where everyone should be dressed meagerly
and less attractively. People will hate the
ugly and not stand up for the weak or fat if
they are not attractive; study sociology. To
have us in tee-shirts and women in tight
pants is like a mill-stone around our necks,
socially. Men are assumed to be speaking
with perverted pretenses because of the way
women are seen without the Victorian

dresses that earned them so much respect and now only your superior is allowed to wear a suit when it used to be every commoner. The presentiment is that others will not react on others' behalves to injustice in public by the official arms of the perpetraitors. Do not be surprised, all our clothes are cheaply made overseas now, we are each in thousands of dollars of debt, and this is the way the establishment wants us divided. This may be considered a contradiction to common sense, but the guy who thinks he is attractive and presentable in sweat pants is horribly vain about his physical visage. If you are concerned about conforming, it cannot even be recommended that you wear your Sunday's best to church or to a funeral these days. A request for formal attire nowadays will be met nonchalantly with blue-jeans and a polo or sweater because people are not taught to respect themselves properly anymore.

Social Security recipients are now trapped in a system that is becoming insolvent. Thankfully, there is a safe solution to this before the Administration is drained of its resources. People do not have to be powerless who have paid into the program when it is only able to pay a portion of the promised benefits in the future. Privatization was previously touched upon where those paying into Social Security would have the option to invest part of their hard earned money to increase what they receive. There is also another solution that politicians should investigate and consider. We do not have to abandon the needs of its recipients if the individual States would supplement the checks like so many already do. For instance, to help beneficiaries cope financially, Wisconsin adds eighty-three dollars a month to SSI. When the Federal government absolutely cannot keep up with this entitlement, each State can ensure that the total monthly amount rewarded does not diminish by adding a supplemental Social Security check and by increasing the amount of pre-existing supplements. Believe it or not, this is not risking anything more than having to face State tax increases that could be more efficiently spent than Washington's. There is no question that it has more debt per capita than any State and if one or several States fail to take-on the responsibility sufficiently, at least that will not be the entire country sinking, at once. Eventually, the Social Security check could be limited to the approximate amount the State supplements now and then the States can take on most of the burden. Then the giant bureaucracy that eats up Social Security taxes can disappear. Also, to solve the problem more thoroughly, the States could ask the counties to share the burden first and then next even the townships as long as the poorer areas are able to keep some similitude of benefits with the more affluent and populous regions. The cost of living in the poorer areas is lower, so this would not be a problem once local control is launched or more correctly, restored to the care of indigents.

The perpetraitors are actively seeking ways for the American public to be further manipulated. Communications are vital to this effort and the Perpetraitors have managed to conjure up fears of war and fears of a global cataclysm from nuclear weapons for opposing the Communists. Millions are now tormented daily with exaggerated anxieties about the environment's future, claiming we are all going to die and scurrying about with over the top Earth friendly actions to busy themselves. They have created a meaningless controversy where people protest a tree being cut down even though there are more trees than ever before in our country. The roots of all of this are the pagan worship of nature as being spiritual and high schools even have clubs named after the feminine goddess Gaia who is supposedly Mother Earth. They have dismally spread their anti-business propaganda and the latest thing is to ban plastic straws and discourage the consumption of meat.

The PerpeTraitors have been on a mission to dismantle the foundations of American institutions like they are members of the KGB. One of the Communists' goals here was to render artistic expression as useless, so that its spectators could not eventually distinguish the modern art from, trivial and worthless pieces. If the people had nothing of value in their culture, they could be made to bow before Communism easily. Observe the statues of antiquity and compare them to anything, after the Soviet Union, here in America and one must come to the realization that this attack was successful. Now anything abstract or whatever is art like the award winning blank portrait with ketchup splashed on it or a banana duct taped to canvas that went for over a hundred grand. Art promoters focus on complete pieces of trash to exhibit, like in New York City where a sacrilegious statue of Mary or like a bottled cross with urine were on display. However revolting, it is accepted by the Leftist establishment and the artists are talentless with no effect to conceal their lack of taste because of these Perpetraitors. There are now peculiar looking monstrosities somehow labelled as sculptures like a huge and ugly orange thing that the city of Rockford, Illinois wasted its money on. It should be pointed out that they are using racism as an excuse to tear down beautiful statues of anyone who owned slaves or was involved in the Confederacy showing their lack of appreciation for history. Somehow a statue of General Lee that a thousand people came to defend was deemed discriminatory and replaced with abstract shapes that are not appealing to the eye. Anything that gives reference to Southern veterans of the Civil War is being removed or covered by black curtains. Incessant mobs have disrespected these memorials through vandalism or destruction because they think this art is dangerous. A century ago, every piece of modern art would have been rejected and it makes one wonder if anyone is even capable of making a life-like portrait anymore. The object of all of this was to weaken our morale as a people.

In order to subjugate us completely, all they have to do is ignore the Constitution and the Bill of Rights. Presently, most people ignore these documents while formulating their opinions, unfortunately. The author has made the numerous ways even the politicians have ignored it apparent already. Having Congress vote on war before the President acts is now unknown. By the way, there is no confusion about how Congress has the power to declare war by Constitutional law. They have purposely contributed to the Constitution's demise and have ensured the obliteration of our checks and balances. Executive Orders have now become notorious for being limitless and without the support of our elected representatives. The President was to direct the Armed Forces after Congress declared war and to possibly veto bills, serving as an interruption to anything passing through that is un-Constitutional. The Supreme Court is now thought to possess this power, solely, which is not its stated purpose in the Constitution and the Executive Branch's increase in power has been continuous, as well. Until the bicameral Legislative Branch stands up to these usurpations on its bodies, expect a perpetuation of the status quo. The Executive Branch has corrupted the Constitution by signing international agreements when it dictates that the Senate must ratify all treaties by a two-thirds majority. Who is to enforce the laws when it is recognized that the Federal government breaks them? Should it receive discipline by the States or the people; it is like they virtually have no comprehension of the Constitution because the Perpetraitors control all of the textbooks, newspapers, stations, etc.? How far has the public been removed from the concept that our Federal government has been restricted from certain actions by its founding document?

Due to these Perpetraitors the centralized government will be abominable. Any links or favors it gives to the international bankers needs to be abandoned. Jefferson, Jackson, and many other famous leaders have raised objections against their greediness at the expense of the people. We have deserved better and have had it. Americans have been seduced by the international bankers and if we get rid of the Federal Reserve and give the money back to State banks, we could eradicate our budget deficits and have a surplus. We could get out of our seemingly un-removable debt. These people are corrupt and have world conquest on their minds through the control of our leaders. All America will do is incur more debt unless we break the chains of these manipulators of our economy. The benefits of eradicating the international banking system are manifold. For the sake of our posterity, we must end all usury on our nation and only charge interest on foreign nations. We are strong enough to offer interest free loans to our people who are poor. If one views this as an absurdity to a bank's survival, maybe one should consider that they could raise revenue through higher account fees and ATM withdrawal fees instead of eating away at our people's substance. Once these higher fees are exchanged for the banning of interest on our brothers, corporations will become less popular because they will still be charged interest on loans where sole proprietors will not be. Populists need to revive the old stigma that was attached to the banks because they are parasites to productivity and we should never have our government bail them out again.

We have not had a cessation from war for twenty years, although the operations have been light in comparison to other conflicts. We have pierced the backbone of the terrorist in the Middle East by maintaining a continuous presence in that theater of the globe. These dreadful members of the Islamic State cannot be classified as perpetraitors because they are not Leftist and are not betraying our country as traitors, but are its outright enemies. However fearless these terrorists can be with their desperate suicide missions and beheading of Christians, perpetraitors do defend their sympathizers. Expectations would be that all Americans would stand united against them, but now Democrats are complaining about a Special Forces airstrike against one of their military leaders in Iran. Muslims are characterized by their devoutness, but they have responded by launching missiles at an Iraqi base with American connections. Now we are at risk of a war as this book is coming out. The enemy is draining us of our resources, we having spent more money over in the Middle East than is even comprehensible. There should be indignation against the perpetraitors who are preventing us from ruling these people as colonists and acquiring their oil fields as compensation. One grievance that the perpetraitors have with this country is that the USA is imperial because the Communists accuse us of this. Why not totally become an empire, since they already think we are anyways? Besides, what did they consider the miserable USSR that took over Eastern Europe?

To think of all the pains workers go through to put bread on their table while others sit their idly watching television receiving everything for free. I heard that actually thirty-three percent of working-aged adults are not employed, but are not included in the unemployment figures and this is cause for us to mourn. A few of them sit in the lap of luxury, some of them are stay at home moms, and people on Social Security are not included in the numbers. So when Trump would like for some of these people on the check suspected of being ready for work to be interviewed by professionals, he is accused of taking benefits away from the disabled. How is that even an honest evaluation of his intentions when all he is doing is investigating fraud? This is the nature of the media, to reproach the President as much as possible while ignoring the fact the Social Security is a bust. These reporters act under the pretense of telling the truth when in reality it is all done to make the Conservatives look bad. Their arguments would not stand up in the court of law, but there is no opportunity for the other side to expose the fallacies of the Left to the mainstream. When almost ninety-percent of the newspaper editors are Democrat, one would be naïve to believe a fair opinion is being propagated to the public. This is how these perpetraitors operate unsuspected by those who depend upon the mainstream media for their information. They are noisome about the slightest news story in order to sell their media and public media is, of course, going to be biased in favor of the government because it is funded by such people. It would be sagacious to recognize that all governments have the potential for destruction of innocent life within and without its borders and are the number one threats to our civil rights. The severity of this claim is justified by all we know of the history of governments. The consequence of oppression is the acceptance of a might makes right mentality, but with the Bill of Rights we have bound the strong man. For those not acquainted with our God-given rights, one should read the first Ten Amendments to our Constitution and rely on what one thinks not the perpetraitors or those influenced by them. To stand up for justice and one's rights is not insurrectionary and the use of violence is the very last option if taken, at all, once all patience is extinguished for the democratic process.

The day will dawn when the voters will become shrewd in regards to the PerpeTraitors' tricks. Conservatives have pushed back against their media control by using alternative media on the internet and publishing multifarious books with the truth. There will be bitter grief amongst patriots if our right to bear arms is taken away along with our freedom of speech and religion. The individual States have become feeble in comparison to the awesome power of the Federal government and the balance must be restored. Just because the PerpeTraitors have become halfway successful with their

Communist ideology does not mean that Conservative victories are not possible. If we finally get a chance to reform the government, everyone will realize why and afterwards we will not get fooled again. To the perpetraitors let us say, the truth shall make you free. If presented with this book, they should be able to divine all of their misdoings and what they culminate in. They would have the American public blindfolded to common sense about their liberties and executed eventually for defending them. Let us hope that the Democrats in control will no longer shield the gang Antifa from arrest and let us provide ourselves with positive change while preserving the foundations of our freedom.